The only problem with this c̲ ̲‗‗‗‗ᴜᴏᴎ ᴏᴛ Roddy Phillips' humourous columns is that its almost impossible to put down!
Scotland on Sunday

Roddy Phillips' columns offer a gentle and humourous escape from the daily grind and remind readers to see the fun in the everyday. *The Press & Journal*

With a flair for charming self effacement and no scruples about airing slightly grubby laundry, Roddy Phillips regales us with a catalogue of anecdotes and escapades ranging from the hilarious to the cringeworthy and skillfully makes the most everyday, even banal, occurrence an entertaining spectacle.
Ingenue Magazine

Don't read this book in public, not unless you want to look like a laughing loony!
The Scotsman

Lost for Words

Dedicated to my family
without whom it would all be about me.

First Published by Bourne to Write
Kindle - July 2015

Paperback Edition November 2019

Front cover painting "Clown' by Catriona Millar
catrionamillar.com

Aforethought

Since the late 1980's I've written about my family life and times in humorous columns for various newspapers and magazines, including the grand old Scottish morning newspaper The Press & Journal. To my amazement the columns proved quite popular and they were first published in book form in 2009 under the title, 'The Familiar' by the Edinburgh publisher Black & White.

Like all the best career moves the idea of writing a 'living autobiography' happened by accident. The first column was written to fill an unexpected hole in a newspaper. The deadline was tight so I used what was to hand, namely my family's move to the country, an event we are still recovering from. Before I knew it one column had turned into a thousand.

Most writers would have something better to do, but the truth is, when you get paid to air your dirty linen in public, it becomes addictive. Lost for Words was the first collection to appear in Kindle book format and the columns date from 2000 to 2002. Most of them are set in rural Scotland, which explains a lot.

Roddy Phillips

Lost For Words

I've been considering taking up hypochondria professionally. For a small fee I could share my years of extensive moaning with novice whiners. I thought group sessions would be the thing, so everyone could pass their imaginary ailments around and pool them like a fictitious bug bank. My clients would of course be mostly men. Women tend to go for the real thing.

Unfortunately over the past few months I've hit a snag – I've developed a genuine complaint more nebulous than anything I could ever have conjured up and it's hampering me from spreading the news, because I'm literally lost for words.

Around midday my throat goes into auto-edit and whole sentences disappear without trace. This leaves me sounding like a temperamental microphone and whoever I'm speaking to wondering if they've gone intermittently deaf.

Since a good cough normally startles my words back into life I diagnosed a throat infection. So I went to see my GP to share my conclusions with her.

You can imagine my surprise when she contradicted me and said she couldn't find the slightest trace of an infection. I suggested she take a closer look but she was adamant there was nothing there.

I was about to tell her that for once I wasn't over reacting or imagining my symptoms when right on cue I went mute again and mouthed at her like a goldfish.

This was a complete disaster I thought, just when I genuinely have something wrong with me I can't even cry wolf.

She decided a few simple voice tests were in order and when I failed them she nodded sagely and decided I had voice fatigue. I had to take her word for it, because I couldn't find any of mine.

At some point, she said, I must have strained my voice box and now my vocal cords weren't coming up to scratch. But something obviously was, because my throat had a strange peculiar itch.

When she asked if I spoke a lot I had to think about that for a minute while I tried to define what she meant by 'a lot'. I hadn't thought of myself as a chatterbox so in the end I just shrugged my shoulders.

"That's a good start." She said, then joked about writing a prescription telling me to 'shut up'. Instead she prescribed a throat spray and said I would have to see a specialist. Which I was quite excited about.

There's always at least one person coughing in our office apart from myself so the more I thought about it the happier I became with my condition. If nothing else I was a cut above your run of the sore throat merchant because as far as I knew 'voice fatigue' isn't contagious, not unless you're provoking people to shout back at you.

A week later a card arrived inviting me to attend the exotic sounding Maxilofacial Clinic. This must be serious I thought, before they were sending me to a place I couldn't even pronounce.

"The Maxi what?" everyone said, "That must be serious."

Needless to say, my otherwise dilapidated voice box was on fighting form for my appointment. But then I had taken my doctor's advice and adopted my own personal sign language, which admittedly wasn't up to much on the phone.

However, even although my vocal cords were on their best behaviour the specialist wasn't having any of it. I could see him thinking, 'I'll be the judge' as he studied my notes. Then he asked if I shouted a lot. Again I had to think about this so he tried to help me out.

"Some people have to shout a lot...for example, at work," he said, narrowing his eyes suspiciously.

I told him that in my experience shouting at work didn't make it go away, in the end you still had to do it.

He didn't laugh either when I told him my GP suggested writing a prescription telling me to shut up, but the nurse did and then quickly found something better to do.

It was the first time in months I wished my voice had deserted me. During the uncomfortable stony silence that followed I sat in the unnecessarily big chair like a five-year-old and decided I would do as I was told.

So when the specialist asked me to stick my tongue out as far as it would go I was happy to oblige. It's not every day you get the chance to stick your tongue at a specialist, but in the light of what was about to happen I wouldn't recommend it.

Quite naturally, I assumed he was going to examine it. This was nothing new to me. My acupuncturist Fan Zhou was fond of reading my tongue and once showed me a big book of horrible tongues just to keep me awake at night. But instead the specialist took hold of my tongue using a sterile paper napkin and pulled it out a lot further than you can ever imagine.

He did explain what he was doing but I was in no position to comment. When he told me to sing out of tune so he could observe my voice box with a little mirror I was delighted to make any sound at all.

At least I thought I was in an expert hand, and in a way I did feel sorry for him. After all, what kind of job is that, handling a stranger's tongue?

The whole painful process only lasted a few minutes but it couldn't end quick enough for me. When the specialist eventually let go of my tongue I was convinced it wasn't going to spring back to its usual size. Instead I would have to walk around for the rest of life wearing my tongue as a tie.

While I was wondering what colour of shirt would best set it off the specialist suggested I might like to put my tongue back but I still wasn't so sure. I just kept staring down at it because it was now jutting out under my nose like a pink fleshy gangplank.

I felt like shouting, "what on earth have you done to my tongue?" but of course I couldn't, because when I eventually retracted the thing it had been completely stunned into submission. Apart from anything else it wouldn't fit back into my mouth.

Then it dawned on me; this wasn't an examination it was a cure. But it wasn't. An hour later I was failing miserably to find any sort of words to tell my wife about my experience, so I gave her a demonstration.

"What's wrong?" she laughed, "specialist got your tongue?"

Now of course it's a standing joke. We passed a bloke in the street the other day who was wearing a big pink tie and my wife remarked that he had obviously been to the same clinic.

Meanwhile I'm seeing a voice therapist who's had me hissing like a snake. When she has me speaking in tongues I'll let you know. In 9 point Minion of course.

The Green, Green Grass

My father had a foolproof method for mowing the lawn, which he ceremonially imparted to me at an early age like a treasured family heirloom. It was very simple and involved the word delegation.

"One day son," he said as he showed me the lawnmower, "you too will have your own team of little gardeners." Then he walked off and left me to it.

My parents' lawn was only about twice the size of their front room, so small in fact that when I broke the lawnmower while my father was at sea, I cut it with a pair of shears. But you have to remember I was half the size I am now, so it's all relative.

I mentioned this in passing to my son Adam when he broke our lawnmower last week for the fourth time in 18 months. He looked round our half acre of grass and suggested that I should tighten my grip on reality. Apparently I was letting my imagination run away with me again. Then he blamed me for giving him the lawnmower-busting gene in the first place.

When I took the lawnmower down to the repair shop the bloke shouted, "What now?"

He didn't really need to ask because it was exactly the same problem as before – something to do with the starter motor, or in our case the non-starter motor.

It's not that the repairman doesn't want our business but he's asked us to come up with something different next time to make his life more interesting. I told him my son would be happy to oblige.

"I think your son's trying to tell you something," he said shaking his head as he handed me one of those tiny tickets you know you will never see again, "two weeks if you're lucky." He warned.

Personally I think the lawnmower's trying to tell Adam something, like "Take it easy mate."

Anyway, I've done my sums and stumping up for a few repairs, albeit on a regular basis still works out cheaper than hiring a gardener. Although my wife was contemplating it last week when I told her we didn't own a scythe.

She just wanted to hang out some washing without the added excitement of getting kitted out for an expedition into the Bush.

"How long can grass get?" she asked glaring at the foot high washing green with her arms folded, as if a dirty look was going to frighten the grass into submission.

I reckoned on about a week before she cracked and took matters into her own hands.

My father-in-law Ian has also seen the light and hired a gardener. He even has his own lawnmower so Ian thoughtfully handed over his dainty little Flymo. More a plaything really, it looked like it might at a push, or rather a sweep just about cut your toenails.

My wife however, considered herself fully armed for an assault on the washing green and climbed into a huge bright blue boiler suit for the job. As she swaggered off like a miniature hero with her tiny mower I instantly promoted her to head gardener. Not only did she possess a refreshing air of determination but she looked cute and that's an important quality from an audience's point of view.

Unfortunately I had to leave her to it. By the time I came home the back lawn had been transformed into a smooth bowling green carpet, but I think that was mainly because it had been hoovered.

"I'm going to cut the front tomorrow." She said, eyeing up the huge stretch of long grass creeping up to the kitchen window.

I was about to suggest that she was being over ambitious when I remembered my father's foolproof method.

This time when I came home I found a neatly cropped front lawn and what looked like our broken lawnmower resurrected from the dead, but it was far too shiny. There was also a small matter of an uncut stripe of grass right down the middle of the lawn.

"So it's a Mohican!" announced my wife.

Thankfully the replacement lawnmower belonged to our next door neighbours, Sue and Trevor. My wife had borrowed it after the handle snapped off her father's Flymo half way through cutting the front lawn. One moment she was swinging away with the Flymo and the next she was swinging away without it.

In desperation she persisted with what was left of the handle by getting down on her knees and gripping it with all her might but her fingers almost caught fire with the friction. "Why didn't you wear gloves?" I asked.

When I offered to cut the Mohican – it was the least I could do, literally, my wife said she wanted the satisfaction of finishing the job.

Instead she came back and declared that she was retiring to her bed because Sue and Trevor's lawnmower was now broken and it was the safest place she could think of.

At first I refused to believe this was happening but a quick recce round the lawnmower confirmed that it was now dead even though it still had half a tank of petrol.
While I stood and looked nonplussed my wife was hatching a cunning plan to replace Sue and Trevor's lawnmower with an even newer one that still worked.

"Surely they'll know the difference." I protested. But my wife had already thought of this and planned on cutting the rest of the grass with it, "Just to give it some wear and tear." She said, her eyes narrowing deviously.

Before I could stop her she was on the phone to the nearest DIY store informing them that her husband had just bought a green lawnmower that didn't work and that she would like a replacement - without a receipt of course.

When the assistant asked for the make my wife ran outside with the phone and bellowed out anything that was written on the mower. "That's funny," said the assistant, "We don't sell them."

Undeterred my wife tried another store, and another without success.

Just as well, I said as she sat slumped in defeat, for all we knew Trevor had filled the lawnmower handle with rolled up dollar bills – he's American, and he would have been very disappointed when he opened it up to retrieve his stash and discovered it had mysteriously vanished into thin air.

Meanwhile some assistant form the DIY store would have been sunning himself in the Caribbean.

My wife laughed at this and then started praying. Just for good measure she stared very hard at the inert lawnmower with every inch of Witchy power she could muster.

A few minutes later the lawnmower sprang to life at the first tug of its cord. "It's working, it's working!" she screamed just as Sue and Trevor strolled past the garden fence.

Needless to say it was always working, the cord just needed a sharp tug. After giving it the polishing of its life I returned it gleaming to Trevor who squinted at it suspiciously and said, "You sure that's ours, looks as good as new?"

Plugged in

If you're looking for a good night's sleep in a hotel the best time to turn up is around 2.30 am. Only then will the quaint leafy street the hotel brochure describes as 'a perfect hideaway for business or pleasure' reveal its true self and spring into sleep depriving action.

You won't even have to step out of your cab, if the street looks like a cross between an outdoor disco and a fleamarket move on.

Every hotel we've every booked into was like a monastery during the day. Even in rural France or Spain where the noisiest mode of transport was an old donkey, the square outside our hotel turned into party central after lights out.

In Amsterdam my wife and I smiled smugly as we checked into a hotel that overlooked a canal. How noisy could a few barges be, we thought as we unpacked our cases? From our window the coast was completely clear.

Needless to say this turned out to be the noisiest place we had ever stayed. From midnight until daybreak a stadium-sized crowd had the time of their lives outside our hotel. I know because they kept me awake until the meagre sun sent them running for cover.

For some reason my wife was almost immune to it. "Oh it's only a bit of noise." She insisted when I kept accidentally waking her up. The trouble was the hotel room was so hot and badly ventilated we couldn't close the window properly in case we suffocated. Personally I was willing to take the chance but my wife wedged the window open so hard I couldn't budge it without disturbing her.

I even put on a pair of gloves at one point to try and manoeuvre the window silently shut. But it was useless. I felt like a reverse burglar so I went back to bed and tried to pull one of the gloves over my head.

In the morning, despite my wife warning me it was such a middle-aged thing to do I went in search of earplugs. As I staggered through the crowd half asleep I began to think I was recognising some of the revellers that had kept me awake.

I had also convinced myself I would have to trawl the shops of Amsterdam in my quest for a good night's sleep. However, several million tourists had been there before me and the first chemist I tried had an entire display devoted to earplugs.

At first I thought I was spoiled for choice but after browsing through the selection for ten minutes I began to wonder if they were earplugs after all.

I kept picking them up warily and thinking, 'there's no way that's going in my ears'.

I couldn't work out if they were earplugs, suppositories or sex toys, until a pretty blonde assistant appeared. I stuck my fingers in my ears and made a mock yelling noise. The girl laughed and informed me in an accent straight out of Friends that the earplugs were on the other side of the shop.

But still there were dozens of different types to choose from. I was baffled so after a quick recce round my ears the assistant recommended a big fluorescent green pair because I would be able to find them when they fell out.

I told her I didn't want them to fall out and she shrugged her shoulders and said they were designed to fall out.

Call me picky but this didn't seem like a very strong selling point. Anyway I still wasn't convinced they were going to fit my ears in the first place. They were cone shaped and looked big enough to deafen an elephant but I didn't think there was a zoo in Amsterdam so this was difficult to confirm.

The instructions told me to roll and squeeze the end of each earplug to a point before insertion. 'Really!' I thought, 'well that was a handy tip.'

I decided to try them out in the restaurant that evening and although they stuck out of my ears by at least an inch they must have worked because I couldn't hear a thing my wife was saying about me to the concerned waiter.

There were however certain drawbacks. You would almost think that air escaped from my ears because the moment I pushed in the earplugs my head felt as if it began to swell. After about a minute I thought it was going to explode like an over inflated tyre.

It was an alarming sensation. I had never thought of myself as an airhead.

When I pulled out the earplugs I asked my wife, who was still lost in the mysteries of the menu, if my head looked any bigger. She glanced up disinterestedly and said no more than usual.

Later that night I jumped into bed and shoved in my trusty earplugs.

I lay there with my huge head trying to lip read what my wife was saying until finally she pulled out one of my plugs.

"You're not actually going to sleep with those things in are you?" she was shouting.

I explained calmly that was the general idea and that I hadn't just bought them to amuse people in restaurants.

"What if there's a fire alarm? she asked.

"Well, just wake me up," I replied.

She said she would think about it, adding that the earplugs were antisocial. Which I thought was the whole point.

I plugged myself back in and snuggled down for a night of noise-free slumber. 'Come on,' I thought, 'bring on the party animals, do your worst, nothing can touch me now.'

Nothing that is apart from the big old wheezing bellows and the motorbike that revved up every time I so much as twitched a muscle. If I turned my massive airship of a head my highly sensitive earplug antennae went off like screeching sirens inside the over-inflated dome of my skull.

When I pulled one of the plugs free to find out what I was missing, the only noise I could hear was being made by the other earplug rubbing at full volume against my pillow. Obviously the revellers outside were lying low until my earplugs dropped out.

I wasn't taking any chances. In the end the big old wheezing bellows actually sent me off to sleep.

"Maybe that's how the earplugs work." I said to my wife in the morning, "By internalising all the noise."

But apparently they don't internalise every nocturnal noise.

Despite the fact that my wife wanted to confiscate my earplugs pending an authorised Risk Assessment I managed to smuggle them home hidden inside a sock.

I forgot all about them until one day I actually put that sock on. Which was rather handy because even though we live in the heart of the country it can be quite a noisy place at night.

After a recent heavy storm my wife looked at me in the morning and said she couldn't understand how I managed to sleep through it. Like the girl said in the shop, the earplugs are designed to fall out for a reason.

The Agony and The Ecstasy

Right at the very end of a long shopping trip, after I had gazed in mock fascination at pastel coloured kitchen chairs, sniffed a legion of scented candles and tried to pretend I was invisible while my wife fondled an increasing number of identical handbags, I suddenly had this designer kettle thing sprung on me.

Bad news comes in all shapes and sizes I thought, and now even designer kettle shaped.

The strange this was, I was under the delusion that we were on our way back to the car and said as much to my wife. She told me not to worry because by sheer luck the shop with the designer kettles was on the way back to the car.

I wasn't worried, I was sick, my feet were killing me and I thought I had done remarkably well. I deserved to be let off the hook, but there was more agony to come.

The lesson here was, never park your car near shops, least of all in the carpark of a big shopping centre.

As it turned out the kettle shop – actually a big department store disguised as a kettle shop really was on the way to the car, if you were coming from the opposite direction. But then I would have been suspicious if it wasn't.

Apart from her complete lack of directional planning probably the most excruciating thing about shopping with my wife is that more often than not she never buys anything. If she does, it's normally the first thing she saw and she takes it back, sometimes within hours.

If you're a man you might think this is ideal, but in fact being quids in at the end of the day is little comfort.

After window shopping pointlessly for an afternoon all I really want is for my wife to buy something she is completely happy with, anything would do as long as she takes it home and keeps it long enough before thinking about donating it to a charity shop.

Needless to say, I'm missing the point. Because if you buy something and take it back and get a refund, apparently you have won on all counts.

You've enjoyed the experience of shopping – the thrill of the hunt, the ecstasy of trapping your prey and the sensual pleasure of being served by a complete stranger and then you give in, get your money back and it all starts again. If this catches on, shops could be in real trouble.

"But they know already," said my wife, "Why do you think they all have Customer Service departments?"

Whether they know about it or not, I don't think they can be truly prepared for a serial refunder like my wife.

Of course I knew there was more to the designer kettle than she was letting on and I was right. Eventually I was told there was something small that had to be taken back to the same shop, so at least our extra journey wouldn't be wasted. What a relief.

Once inside the department store - named ironically I thought after a man, the ritual of hide and seek began. As an appetiser my wife stepped accidentally onto the downward escalator and sank without trace into the sports department.

She looked up at me in helpless disbelief as she grew steadily smaller and waved a solemn goodbye.

Result, I thought, widescreen TVs. But I'd only got a few feet when my wife rose up alongside me on the return escalator still waving but now wearing a big grin.

"Right, enough entertainment," she announced, "designer kettles!"

Somewhere around soft furnishings our invisible thread snapped and we parted. Just to show that I was mildly interested in looking at a bunch of kettles I made for the kitchen department where I spotted a shelf full of the gleaming things.

I heard this excitable woman shouting in the distance, "Ha, Ha I've found them. I've found them!" and thinking it was my wife trying to turn me into a trained pet, decided that I had also found them.

Some of the assistants at the nearby till were looking round to see what this frantic woman had found, but I was doing my best to pretend that it wasn't me. I was also getting vaguely interested in a £94 kettle. It was certainly way ahead of your run of the mill device for boiling water. But at almost a hundred quid I thought the least they could have done was throw in a plug.

Suddenly I was aware of a figure standing beside me and I was just about to tell my wife about the madwoman screaming across the shop when I realised it was an old friend.

"Twenty five years ago," I began, "this kettle would have cost me a month's salary and it doesn't even have a plug."

Derek peered at the kettle over his specs, "it doesn't have a lead either mate, because it's not electric."

For a moment we gazed in wonder at the most expensive kettle we had ever seen like cavemen on the brink of discovering fire. So there we were, two grown men reduced by our absent wives to playing shops.

"Anyway if you're just going to speak about kettles, I'm off," continued Derek coming to his senses.

I had to plead with him not to leave and then we spoke about business until we both remembered we weren't supposed to be enjoying ourselves.

We went in opposite directions to look for our respective wives and within minutes we had passed one another twice like little lost boys, panic stricken at losing themselves in the big shop. We laughed it off, but we weren't fooling anyone, least of all each other.

This is the real heart of shopping darkness, because now the solitary male could be mistaken for a man that shops and attaching yourself to your wife is ironically the only means of making a respectable, if painfully slow getaway.

When I get lost in shops my wife thinks I'm either being weird or awkward and this worries me, because I don't particularly want to be either. So I try hard to focus on the job in hand and the harder I try the more my mind wanders and my feet follow behind.

In the bedding department I passed a little boy trampolining on a bed while his father sat on the floor reading a comic and I felt dizzy with shame, because basically this was everyman caged by stuff that he has no use for.

When I eventually found my wife - in the Customer Services department she asked if I had heard that strange woman shouting at the kettles.

To be fair my wife can see my point of view, she just doesn't want to encourage it. She admitted that men who are attentive when their wives are stroking fabric samples are either feeling guilty because they're having affairs, or they've married very rich women.

Which puts me completely in the clear.

"Of course," my wife added, "they could just be nice men who enjoy shopping with their wives or partners."

Something to work on I thought.

Odd Man Out

You would be surprised how difficult it is to stand on one foot, particularly when you have to hold your other foot behind you while stretching out your free arm and focussing on the distant, blurred end of your forefinger.

If you can't resist trying it, make sure you're within falling distance of a trusted friend.

It was while attempting this deceptively hard posture that I realised I was the only man in the Hatha Yoga class, apart from the teacher, but he didn't count because he knew what he was doing, and he could have stood on one foot for as long we liked.

As I lost my balance and fell over for the umpteenth time I was never more conscious of being a big daft bloke. According to the teacher it was my concentration I was losing and not my dignity.

Practising this semi-balletic posture is meant to improve your mind control, but I must have been out of my mind doing it in the first place, especially in a room full of women, some of whom like my wife for instance, were mastering the balancing act without so much as a wobble.

The wall length mirror wasn't helping. The infectiously calm and remarkably pliable teacher was standing a few yards in front of me, and I'd already proved that I couldn't tell my left from my right. There was always that embarrassing moment of hesitation when I tried hopelessly to work out if he meant my right, his right, or my right in the mirror.

At the beginning of every posture I did a little two-step dance until I'd sorted myself out. The teacher just smiled and shook his head and shouted, "right side, right side," but it didn't make any difference. Even when I had realised I was the odd man out, facing the wrong way from everyone else in the class; I still couldn't figure it out.

Unfortunately some of the other less experienced Yoga students, thinking they were in the wrong position, started copying me, and I set up a little breakaway group of rebel storks. All we needed was some Bernstein and we would have had a nice little Jets and Sharks thing going.

I had also remembered why I had never considered a career as a ballet dancer. I was too tall and ungainly for a start. Reflected next to the neatly built teacher in the mirror I was like a huge threatening robot. A quick glance behind me confirmed that no one else was faring any better in the mirror stakes and everyone was trying hard to avoid their distorted alter ego.

"You mustn't look in the mirror," scolded the teacher, "you will only upset yourself."

I think he meant unbalance yourself but either way he was right.

Unsurprisingly, the Hatha yoga class had been my wife's idea. A combination of gentle exercise and breathing was how she had pitched it, which in the privacy of our own home didn't sound particularly dangerous.

The Sanskrit word 'ha' means sun and 'tha' means moon, and Hatha Yoga is basically about balancing the opposing parts of the physical body, the front and back, left and right, top and bottom.

I pointed out that I had been breathing quite successfully for some time now - 23,000 times a day to be precise and managing not to fall over, too often, but apparently that wasn't good enough.

"Well Madonna and Geri Halliwell do it," she said, so off we went rejoicing.

Half an hour later I was trying to stand on one foot while gazing intently at the fingertips of my left hand surrounded by giggling women.

At least when the teacher told us that Geri Halliwell had been pictured in the tabloids incorrectly practising that very posture I felt a lot better. In fact I must have come over all smug because I got one of those looks from the teacher that brought me down to earth again, literally with a thud.

The same thing happened during the warm-up when we had to stand on one foot and rotate our ankles. This isn't the sort of thing I would normally do in the course of a day and I was rather alarmed to find that I could rotate my ankles in the first place.

Actually the hardest part of Hatha Yoga is remembering to breathe. While you're mustering every fibre of your body in order to maintain your agonising posture it's easier just to hold your breath and turn yourself into a quivering statue. During the first class this happened more by accident.

At the beginning of every posture we mimicked the teacher as he told us to breathe in, but there was never any mention of breathing out, until the posture was finished. Consequently half the students are now fully trained pearl divers.

At one point while we were engaged in a posture that looked like a form of weird semaphore my wife and I glared at one another like red-faced balloons fit to burst.

"You are breathing during the posture?" asked the teacher as we stood up gasping.

We laughed heartily in reply - as if we'd be that stupid. But the relief was palpable right round the room.

As was the sound of stiff neglected joints cracking. In fact I never realised the human body could be so noisy. At one point as we bent backwards with our hands stretched above our heads and then down again to hold our ankles it was like a great fire crackling.

In between every strenuous posture you assume a special relaxing posture, close your eyes, focus on your breathing and quietly smoulder for a few minutes.

The teacher told us that eventually he would divulge the secret of how to think about nothing while we were in these postures, which will be a relief to everyone who lay there mentally bombarded with the forthcoming week's shopping lists.

We were then taught how to ritually breathe in one nostril and out the other. Which may not sound too much like a revelation but if you do it for even fifteen minutes it's a lot cheaper than a trip to the off licence.

Before long I had a serene expression to match the teacher's and I was ready for anything. Just as well because we were back in the ballet class again, but this time it was my turn to be the star of the show.

With our hands locked high above our heads we had to stand on our toes and stare up at the ceiling. Much to my amazement, while everyone else danced backwards and forwards I stood riveted to the spot.

Finally I had found my natural posture. Now all I had to do was relax and think about nothing.

However, I must be getting the hang of it. When I demonstrated this astonishing posture to one of our sons he looked at me disdainfully and asked what was for tea and the great thing was I just stood there without a care in the world letting it all wash over me.

The Sandals

You have to be on your guard when out you're out shopping. Last week I walked into a shop stocked entirely with the contents of my Mother's house from 1970. A few items might have been excusable but a whole house seemed suspiciously like a deliberate act of style irony.

I can't remember what the shop was called but it should have had a sign outside with my parents' old address on it.

It was the big purple goblet vases in the window that stopped me. Inside, through the glass bead curtains, I could see dozens of fashionable young people pouring earnestly over fibre optic lamps and psychedelic cushions.

At first I wondered if it was an art gallery - sometimes it's difficult to tell these days, but the main thing was, I was interested and hooked, mainly because I thought, 'here was something I know about'.

How right I was. Just a few feet inside the door I turned into Dorian Gray confronted by his notorious portrait. Except in reverse. While I had been buffed and buffeted by the years, my past life was still horrifyingly bright, shiny and new. Although the fact that most of it was synthetic was certainly some comfort.

An enthusiastic assistant bounced up in a green and yellow Paisley pattern trouser suit and asked if she could help. But I was speechless so she bounced quickly across to a couple who were mulling over some mushroom lamps - they couldn't decide between the aluminium or matt black base.

Meanwhile I stood there looking as if I had been mugged several hundred times over and the security guard on the door didn't even flex a muscle.

Actually I couldn't make up my mind what was more alarming - seeing all these unnaturally coloured plastic objects again, or realising that they were brand new and then worrying about the fact that someone had actually bothered to make them for the second time round and dedicate a whole shop to selling them.

By the time my wife found me I was in a deeply confused state of chronic nostalgia exacerbated by the sound of Marc Bolan urging me to Ride a White Swan.

"Oh," was all my wife said, but it spoke volumes. She obviously knew this sort of thing had been going on, and as we gazed round in silent awe at the shelves of orange and purple ornaments and vibrant swirling fabrics she could barely conceal her guilty expression.

"It's only stuff," she said fixing me with a sympathetic stare.

She was right of course and I was on the brink of agreeing with her when a young girl passed carrying a lava lamp up to the counter and I almost shouted out, "hey where do you think you're going with my Mum's lamp?"

But my wife gripped my arm and reminded me that we were in a shop and that it was perfectly legal for complete strangers to buy up the thirty-year-old contents of my mother's house.

This was the worst part - watching people scrutinising my parents' furniture and cherished knick-knacks and knowing that they could take them back to a strange place where someone would declare them to be 'totally cool'.

"It's a compliment really," said my wife, as we stood in front of my mother's white laminated TV set on which was playing a video of Are You Being Served? - my mother's favourite programme.

This was too spooky for words. Any minute now my mother would turn up and say, "Do you think my hair is the same colour as Mrs Slocombe's?"

Purple was my mother's main theme colour; the orange was really just an accent.

Upstairs we found my mother's clothes – the mini-dresses and trouser suits with gold medallion belts, the big flowery floppy hats and rows and rows of kinky boots. Neil Diamond was singing Cracklin' Rosie and I was feeling faint.

Back outside in the busy street we were laughing about it but the experience had burrowed into me and I was about to flush it out in the strangest way.

Half an hour later after finding my mother's thirty-year old kitchen in Habitat I was gripped by a sudden, inexplicable urge to buy sandals and headed for the nearest shoe shop. My wife followed behind shouting, "sandals?" over and over again but I couldn't explain it.

In the shop while a completely spaced-out young girl wearing one of my old tank tops and a pair of my mother's plastic hoop earrings went in search of size ten sandals my wife stood over me with her arms folded and gave me the third degree.

"Is it a Gladiator thing?" she asked squinting at me in an effort to see how I would measure up against Russell Crowe in a short skirt.

The cosmic assistant was back dangling several pairs of sandals in front of me so I couldn't give my wife the answer she deserved.

I tried on the left foot of each pair because I was fairly confident that I had a large hole in the big toe of my right sock and after a brief mental tussle I announced a winner.

But my wife still wasn't happy and demanded that I try on both the sandals of each pair and parade myself in front of a floor length mirror for the entertainment of the entire shop.

She was very insistent about this and for one horrible moment I was back shopping with my mother and I realised why I was buying sandals.

They were a symbol not only of my childhood, but also of my hippie teenage years. Like my mother's ornaments and groovy objet d'art they were vital props from the film of my past that I constantly replay and re-edit.

I shared this with my wife and she said I didn't have to try on both the sandals if I didn't want to. There was also mention of my favourite pudding being on the menu that evening.

I felt much better after I had bought the sandals; so much so that I never had to wear them, in fact my wife took them back a few days later and got a refund.

The main thing was after I had bought the sandals I felt I could go back and rescue a souvenir from the shop selling my mother's stuff. Before I knew it I had bought a plastic orange table lamp that has now become my favourite security blanket.

It is also the first household object I have ever bought in my life and my wife is still reeling from shock. Actually I think she's worried about what I'm going to buy next now that I've broken through that barrier.

"What on earth are you going to do with that?" she asked, closing her eyes with horror as I pulled the lamp from its box and dusted it down.

I took the hint and gave it pride of place in my study where it now glows in the evening like a big orange spangle that also somehow rather magically, lights up the past.

The Painful Truth

My dentist has been on a journey to the centre of my head. I hate to think what she found there but she is welcome to it. She has certainly earned it after putting up with my moaning and whining for the best part of ten days.

I've no doubt it was a fascinating odyssey of Jules Verne proportions, jam packed with incident and antibiotics, but there were times when I would have been quite happy to leave her to get on with it.

In fact, I just wanted to leave full stop. Particularly when the going got tough and the urge to be somewhere else became almost uncontrollable.

The first bolt of pain caught me completely off guard because my face was frozen solid, and you don't expect that sort of thing when your head feels like a ventriloquist's doll that you've been left in charge of.

Later, I began wondering if inanimate objects, like chopping boards or frying pans, felt pain and I made a mental note never to slam a door or kick the lawnmower again.

The dentist did warn me about the second onslaught of pain which was very nice of her I thought, but there was still nothing I could do about it. I hadn't mastered the ventriloquist act so I couldn't tell her I'd changed my mind about the whole thing, or remembered a pressing engagement several miles away.

This didn't stop me from attempting to leave however, so to prevent myself from bolting through the door I decided I had to take the dentist's chair with me and then tried to rip it up from the floor with my bare hands.

This would have been a neat trick if I could have managed to manoeuvre it down the stairs, while still sitting in it. But it wouldn't budge, even though I made the veins on the backs of my hands stand out like tree roots.

So I had to content myself with trying to rip the chair's arms off while my dentist plunged on into uncharted territory, like a determined pot holer.

Something for me to squeeze that eventually exploded, without doing any harm of course, would have been ideal at this point. The boffins at dentist HQ should be working on this.

"That's just a typical male reaction to pain." Advised my wife later when I blubbed out the whole sorry tale, 'Nothing to be ashamed of."

"But it was unbelievable and it was bright electric blue." I told her, as if that was going to make any difference, "Like an enormous lightning bolt that erupted in my head then ran all over me. I actually broke out into a sweat. It was terrible."

My wife looked sympathetic but I don't think she believed me, probably because I also told her I'd had a local anaesthetic and that the injection, which seemed to burrow its way up into my left eye socket, made my eyes water.

In the waiting room, as my face froze over, my eyes continued to water and drip all over my OK! magazine, smudging 32 perfectly posed pictures of Michael Douglas and Catherine Zeta Jones gazing lustfully at one another over their new baby.

By the time I was back in my dentist's chair my head was so numb I could have been Catherine Zeta Jones for all I knew. Which of course made the pain all the more astonishing.

I was so surprised I didn't think it was my pain at all. It was a new one on me and it definitely felt as though it belonged to someone else. Perhaps, I thought, I was simply looking after it, while they were busy having a nice time - "Keep an eye on that pain for me will you?"

When they came back to collect their stupid big pain I would be having some serious words with them.

This all started with a much smaller pain which, as my dentist struck gold again and I shot up towards the ceiling, I was now beginning to remember fondly.

What fun that little pain and I had, chasing one another around the house and the office, playing hide and seek, scaring me in the middle of the night and sneaking up on me in the car with all its cheeky mates and making me almost drive up the back of a bus.

My wife recommended Sinusitis, which I was happy to have, better than toothache any day. Held up, as principal piece of incriminating evidence was the little pain's ability to move around in a quirky and playful manner.

It also had a preference for the left side of my face, admittedly it preferred all of it and it had every last one of my teeth in its thrall, but I was coping admirably, I could still eat baby food with the other side of my mouth and drink through a straw.

So this was no problem, I had no other symptoms of Sinusitis but I wasn't fussy, because at least it wasn't toothache. When people asked why I looked and talked as if I had an invisible axe through my head I told them it was my sinuses. "It's not infectious is it?" they all asked in a growing chorus of alarm.

It took me four pain-discoloured days to admit I was in denial, but even then my finger hovered over the phone between the doctor's number and the dentist's.

In the end the dentist won because her surgery is two minutes from my office and she agreed to see me within the hour.

"I'm fairly certain I'm wasting your time." I said climbing onto her chair, "I think its Sinusitis, spreading down my face like a pain that just resembles toothache."

My dentist smiled sympathetically, but I could see her thinking, "Ah, Dr Phillips I presume..."

She didn't waste any time, after a quick squint she tapped the big front tooth on the left side of my mouth and I went into orbit for 24 hours. The incredibly painful journey was about to begin, but first there was a preface, a scene setter:

Basically the big front tooth that was now shrieking like a chainsaw was on its last legs, and had started a bacterial infection, just for spite and my immune system had sent in the troops, the white blood cells.

As a result of this microscopic scrap, foul-smelling pus had formed within the tooth pulp and set up an agonising chain reaction that could only be broken by intervention. My dentist would have to go in and stop the fight. A local anaesthetic would help, but it still wouldn't prevent me from catching a lot of the flak.

"So there's no chance it could be my sinuses?" I asked, hopefully.

My wife bought me a present. A goldfish called Gilbert in a glass ball that sparkles when you shake it. But when you pick it up the glass turns out to be jelly and it shrinks in your hand.

"It's a metaphor," she explained cheerfully, "for self-deception."

I'll always treasure it.

Don't Panic

My wife has a habit of keeping her outdoor clothes on when she does the cooking. In the winter this could be a big coat, scarf, hat and gloves. When the kitchen heats up she just throws open the windows so that every corner of the house fills with unexpected icy blasts. Then she says she has to keep her coat on because our house is always so cold.

Sometimes she'll walk about like this for hours, so you never know if she's coming or going. I used to find this unsettling. It was like living with a refugee who was permanently in transit, but now I don't mind because at least my wife is low-maintenance in the wardrobe department.

Although I am slightly concerned that one evening she will turn up at the opening of some swanky gallery, or a first night at the theatre wearing the remnants of our evening meal as jewellery.

The kitchen coat usually means there's a panic on, a tight deadline to meet that doesn't allow for a quick change. Sometimes I think she just forgets, because I can come home for tea, go out and review a show at a theatre, phone it in and put my feet up three hours later and she still has the coat on.

Last Wednesday teatime it was definitely panic stations. She was feverishly chopping vegetables in her favourite black coat while intently listening to the news on the radio, and it wasn't good. The fuel crisis was turning into a food crisis; some supermarkets had introduced rationing while others already had empty shelves.

The irony of supermarket executives pleading with their customers not to bulk buy was too good to be true. It must have hurt them to do it. There must have been deep intakes of breath and much weeping in the stock room afterwards.

The trouble is the very word panic, causes panic. From what I could see the whole thing had a distinctly Dad's Army feel to it. On the one hand we had Captain Manwairing types on TV detailing the positions of the blockades and panic merchants screaming, 'Don't panic, don't panic!'

Basically we were at war, a situation confirmed by older members of the community who admitted sagely that they'd seen it all before.

My wife had seen it all before as well - 150 years ago during the Irish potato famine. Apparently she has been genetically modified over generations to react very quickly to potential grub shortages.

Somewhere in her DNA there is a tiny scribble of code that sounds the mother of all alarm bells when anyone so much as whispers the word rationing.

"The survival of the fattest," I suggested, but she was too focussed for levity. There was food to prepare, and store, and most important of all, bread to bake.

I've never shared my wife's enthusiasm for bread and I know it's very big on the continent but it's just bread, and frankly it can be rather, bread-like.

I wondered if she could bake something more interesting, like some big cakes, but it was all about bread.

"I'll have to get some bread mix!" she proclaimed, then added darkly, "guard those pots with your life."

Then she was off to the village shop, which she said would be under siege by a pack of frenzied shoppers.

"I may be some time!" she shouted over her shoulder, as I prepared to stand watch over the cooker.

I've never guarded Brussels sprouts before so I wasn't sure about the drill. After about ten minutes I decided nothing very much was happening so I switched on the TV to look at the rows of bare supermarket shelves and kicked myself for not giving my wife a list. It was probably only a short time before Off-licences ran dry and events took a rather sober turn.

Up at the local shop apparently everything was suspiciously normal. There were no big queues of exasperated shoppers, but there was also no bread mix and no yeast, so my wife had to content her self with an extra large load of flour and two tins of Carnation milk - for the desperate hours I was assured.

The girl in the shop was fascinated to hear about my wife's plan to bake for Scotland, and wondered what the bread would be like without yeast.

"Probably a bit like a pizza base," my wife admitted. The girl couldn't wait to sample some, but was going on holiday in a few days so my wife promised to keep some for her.

I still refused to go into full panic mode, but driving home from a theatre through the city later that night I wasn't laughing.

At ten o'clock the streets were spookily deserted. It was like breaking a curfew. Even the buses had stopped running.

As I passed garage after garage that had run out of petrol and the occasional car abandoned by the roadside, I began to wish I had started that vegetable patch I've been putting off for six years. There was always the rabbits, I thought, they could keep us going for months.

On the dual carriageway I was frantically trying to work out how I was going to siphon petrol out of my lawnmower. I reckoned there had to be at least half a litre, and I pictured myself going into the office the next day, in fact everyone going into the office the next day, a walking fire hazard with petrol breath.

I even began to wonder how far I could get driving the lawnmower into town. I could stop off and do a few lawns on the way and make a few bob. It wasn't exactly Mad Max but it was the best I could come up with.

Unfortunately I relayed all this to my wife who the following day was up at the crack of dawn and heading for the nearest supermarket. The coat was obviously going to be on for the rest of the day.

Later she phoned me to tell me she had everything in control and that people weren't taking the situation seriously because the supermarket aisles had been almost deserted and the shelves were still creaking with food. There was also no rationing, or at least none that she could find. It was a disgrace.

She had been expecting the last minute Christmas Eve rush mob, but instead she sauntered round in blissful isolation buying absolutely anything she fancied, mostly bread mix as it turned out. Luckily she also resorted to type and went into Hogmanay shopping overload, so now we have enough alcohol and snacks to re-stage the global millennium party.

My wife has also discovered she can bake bread that wouldn't kill you if it landed on your head and the chore of filling up with fuel in a smelly gale-tossed petrol station has now been transformed into a birthday-sized treat.

Life may be returning to normal but my wife remains dressed for action, at all times of the day, and bread mix will always be top of our shopping list, next to petrol of course.

The Family Anthem

I was reviewing a production of Joseph and the Amazing Technicolor Dreamcoat recently and as usual I found myself singing along. Nothing too enthusiastic, more a gentle reverie, which was just as well.

We had reached the scene where Pharaoh in the guise of Elvis – who else? sings about his strange recurring dream and Joseph, being a right little know-all steps up and interprets it as an omen of the seven years of rich harvests and the seven years of famine that will follow.

It's a big glitzy number for the entire cast, but it's not exactly one of the show's most famous songs. Nevertheless, this is where I joined in with "Seven years of bumpercropalopalis, seven years of boom de croom..."

If you've seen the musical Joseph, or simply have a glint of common sense, you'll know that no one would have paid Tim Rice to write lyrics like this. For a start they're difficult to remember, never mind the fact that they don't make any sense.

This has never bothered me because it was our youngest son Adam who inflicted them on me.

When he was six or seven years old Adam used to broadcast the nightly television news live from his bath, using a bottle of shampoo as a microphone.

These bath time broadcasts were dazzling, farcical parodies, usually based around the hilarious adventures of Mrs Thatcher, whom Adam had adopted as an honorary auntie, honorary because she was really Sue the stuffed panda's auntie.

Sometimes bottles of bath salts or bars of soap would be held up for a quick vox pop, and quite often there would be technical hitches when Adam in a fit of over-enthusiasm, momentarily lost his Vosene shampoo microphone under the water. Sue the panda and a very plump bear called Bumper used to sit and watch all this completely non-plussed from the top of the cistern.

One evening in the bath, after he had rounded up the soapy headlines with Mrs Thatcher being blown into space, (he did requests) Adam announced with his usual inflated pomp that he would be finishing the evening's show with a selection of his latest hits.

I wasn't all that familiar with the musical Joseph so when he let rip with "Seven years of bumpercropalopalis..." I was none the wiser.

I suppose I must have thought it was a song about Bumper the bear, but really I had no idea. Whatever it was I couldn't quite get my brain round it. For one thing it wasn't a whole song; it was more of a chorus repeated over and over until you went blue in the face, or fell asleep.

After hearing this peculiar number another four dozen times the whole family was singing it in unison. You couldn't help it; the tune just stuck in your head and refused to budge. It became our family anthem, a song to be sung for no other reason than it was fun and it made us laugh.

Driving around in the car, walking down the road or playing in the park we would erupt into a spontaneous round of the 'Bumper' song, as it became known.

As public performances became more frequent I found I had to resist the temptation of taking part. For instance I refused to join in when we were in shops, or whispering it in the library and I never sang it to train ticket inspectors or supermarket check-out assistants, thus earning me something of a reputation of a boring old windbreak.

My wife and I were always a little troubled about the lyrics, but after years of watching Children's television we would have believed anything. At one point I tried to write them down but gave up when a colleague in the office caught me and panicked because he thought I'd turned dyslexic.

One day Adam arrived home from school and announced we had to make some costumes. He didn't tell us exactly what they were for, 'just a show' I think he said and so we assumed they were for his news programme and were only too happy to see him move his broadcasts onto dry land.

However, once he started detailing what was involved in the costumes, we did wonder if he was going into religious programmes, because they seemed a touch on the biblical side, if not downright Old Testament.

A few white sheets, a false beard and a ratty wig did the trick. Next he was choreographing the Bumper song; or rather we were all choreographing the Bumper song. This went down a treat in the supermarket. Certainly from where I was hiding it looked great.

I think at some point when our children were small my wife must have got it into her head that we were The Partridge Family. If we had taken it more seriously we would be doing a comeback tour of Japan right now.

A few weeks later at a theatre we met one of Adam's teachers quite by chance. She asked how Adam was coming along rehearsing the show, "I hope he's learned all his lines." She said, and we nodded and smiled in blissful ignorance.

Now it all made sense, the songs, the costumes, the dancing, everything had been for a school show. The end result obviously wasn't as important to Adam as the preparation. But it was to us, and so we began rehearsing seriously.

I wanted to see a script but Adam didn't know which part he was meant to be playing and he said he didn't have any lines, but that he might make some up. However, he was word perfect on the Bumper song and that was the main thing.

The week of the show I put Adam in a TV commercial and he missed a rehearsal, his teacher didn't believe him or me when I explained, and sacked him from the show. Her musical it seemed was bigger than my film shoot.

So in the end we didn't get to see Adam play fourth goat herder, or hear him sing his Bumper song in harmony with thirty-three other Old Testament midgets.

Consequently for years we went around chanting that song totally oblivious that we should have been singing, "Seven years of bumper crops are on their way, seven years of endless wheat and tons of hay, your farms will boom there won't be room to store the surplus food you grow."

The revelation finally came when I reviewed Joseph the musical for the first time. Everything was fine until we reached that scene with Elvis Pharaoh, and then my wife and I burst out laughing. We could hardly believe it. They were singing our song, but with the wrong words, 'what a cheek'! we chorused.

The strange thing is we still believe our version is the original. Inadvertently Andrew Lloyd-Webber and Tim Rice gave us a great gift, albeit filtered through the naïve, but inventive mind of our son Adam.

For us it holds a precious moment in our past, frozen forever in complete nonsense. As far as we are concerned they definitely don't write them like they used to.

All in a Good Cause

I make a point of never volunteering for anything, because I know that it's only a matter of time before my wife does it for me. In otherwords I do what I'm told. This gives me the comfort of occupying the moral high ground without actually knowing where it is.

In the past, this sort of thing would happen without me even noticing it. One minute I would be asked to hold a dripping paintbrush while my wife washed her hands, and the next there would be a queue of thespians forming to thank me for volunteering to paint their panto set.

After years of finding myself inextricably sacrificed to a good cause I still can't find a way out, but I have at least developed an early warning system, which allows me the fantasy of running away. Its signal is the deceptively innocent sounding phrase; "it won't take a minute".

If you're my wife, then it really won't take a minute, because that's all the time she needs to involve me.

My wife says this is simply a matter of management and delegation. She finds something that needs to be done, which she discovers she can't manage and then delegates me.

We were on our way home last week from a shopping trip when that fateful phrase reared up and engulfed me like a tidal wave.

"Do you mind if we stop and collect some stuff on the way home?"

"Of course, no problem." I said. Harmless enough I thought. But then right out of nowhere came, "It won't a take a minute."

My wife muttered it as she rummaged in her handbag for an ominous sounding piece of paper. These were obviously our directions and the muttering was just her way of saying they would soon belong to me.

As we drove in ever widening circles towards this 'stuff it would just take a minute to collect'; I attempted to cheer myself up with the prospect of embarking on a new great worthy adventure. What would this 'stuff' consist of, I thought. The excitement was killing me. So much so that I could barely concentrate on where I was going.

My wife of course had excellent directions written on her piece of paper, and although she was holding it upside down, it was me who had got us lost.

Just to make matters worse it was raining heavily; but then it has to rain heavily before my wife can take me on one of her quests.

After passing the house we were looking for three times, which seemed to have been built on the wrong side of the road, we decided we had arrived.

"I suppose it depends on where you're coming from." Consoled my wife. Then she said it again; "This won't take a minute."

And she was right. Obviously she now has this delegation business down to a fine art, because about thirty seconds later she dashed back to the car with a cardboard box under her arm.

She was wet, but absolutely delighted. Apparently there was a lot more where that came from, far too much to fit into her own tiny car, so she wondered if I could collect the rest at my leisure. Since this would be when I retire, I said I would do it the next day.

Peering into the box I tried to work out what was so exciting and important about its contents, but it just looked like old junk to me, and there was lots more of it waiting for me to collect.

"I haven't bought this stuff," countered my wife, "It's for the Imperial Cancer Research shop. I said I would collect stuff for them."

It's always nice to know who I'm working for.

A few days later the front passenger seat of my car was covered in maps. The back seat and the boot were groaning with piles of loose-limbed boxes of books and crockery, bulging black refuse bags that you could barely pick up, a rolled up duvet, an electric blanket, and a sinister gang of soft toys that had been seriously sucked on.

Essentially I was driving a charity shop, and even though it was all in a good cause, I felt like a rag and bone man.

There is something very spooky about sharing an enclosed space with someone else's cast-offs, even more so when they aren't very valuable. This was everyday flotsam, but at some point all these things played an important, or in the case of the re-shaped teddy bear with one ear, vital role in their owner's lives. As I drove around scouting for the next junk donor I wondered if burglars ever donated their unwanted plunder to charity shops, perhaps as a form of restitution.

At least all of my householders were more than happy for me to divest them of their belongings. Although I did wonder why they couldn't just drive down to the charity shop themselves since most of them had cars. In fact some of them had several cars, one had three, including a neat little red sports number.

I had allowed my wife to talk me into this business because she said none of the people could manage to deliver their donations. When I arrived at the Imperial Cancer Research shop I found out why. It was right next to two other charity shops near a busy junction and a set of traffic lights. I had to make three stops just to empty the boot.

I decided I could live with the black bags on the back seat until I had accumulated enough brass neck to revisit the wrath of my fellow motorists.

The next drop was going to be a titanic effort, and I had that sinking feeling before I even set off.

Needless to say it was raining heavily, so I took a leaf out of my wife's book and delegated my son Adam to do the donkey work while I guarded the car a couple of hundred yards away round the corner.

It took Adam three trips but I think he found it a rewarding experience. "It's all in a good cause." I shouted after him as he snarled his way down a flight of steps with two stuffed black bin bags in each hand.

As the boxes disappeared one by one I could feel my car breathing a sigh of relief.

Finally Adam slumped into the passenger seat with a lovely rosy glow on his cheeks. He was now rather pleased with himself because the old lady in the shop was absolutely delighted with such a large and unexpected donation.

He had of course dumped everything in the first charity shop he had come to, which was not exactly the plan. There was nothing else for it. I had to take matters into my own hands and volunteer Adam to go back, explain his mistake, ruin the nice old lady's day and then take everything to the Imperial Cancer Research shop next door.

"It won't take a minute," I said.

The Birds

Sometimes you would get an early warning – a scattering of fluffy feathers that led like a macabre treasure trail to the poor victim. But mostly you came upon them by chance, every one of them bearing the distinctive trademark of their assassin.

A criminal psychologist would have had a field day with this serial murderer, but I doubt they would have got much sense out of it if they had caught it, because hopefully the killer in our midst had four legs.

Purely by innocent association it was my father-in-law Ian who alerted me to the first corpse, I say alerted, but it was more like alarmed.

Ian was having trouble with moss in his front lawn, a patch of grass not much bigger than my car, which looked suitably green to me. But apparently it was the wrong type of green, mossy as opposed to grassy, and Ian wasn't happy.

So he decided to the back of my shed, a place I avoid at all costs. Ian knows the back of my shed better than I do, because half the stuff in it belongs to him. So when he told me I had a contraption for scattering lawn feed I took his word for it.

If I could dig it out, he would use it to lay moss killer and then restore his lawn to exactly the same colour it was at the moment.

"Its got a handle," he added obliquely, "You'll recognise it when you see it."

I wouldn't have laid any bets on it. There was a time in the distant past when I could have recognised the back of my shed.

I can vaguely remember dozens of handy looking things neatly hanging up in rows, but when I opened the door I just thought I was in the wrong shed.

"Some cheeky monkey's using our shed as a furniture store," I told my wife. She didn't like the sound of this and demanded to know why I had been rooting around in the shed. Apparently it had slipped my mind to apply for a shed search permit.

In my defence I blamed her father for wanting to borrow some kind of contraption with a handle on it, which I had never seen before in my life.

"He claims I once burned our lawn with it." I added, chuckling to myself.

Which is why my wife hid it in the pend out of harm's way.

The pend is the covered archway that divides our Steading. In the past, horses, carts and farm machinery would have driven through it, now it's somewhere to go at night when you want the fright of your life, because there's always some wild animal lurking at the end of it.

It's also an extremely effective wind tunnel, so it's ideal for hiding things, like gardening equipment my wife has labelled too dangerous for me to be in charge of.

This particular piece of equipment would be a window box if it didn't have wheels and a handle like a lawnmower's. It took me several turns around the pend in broad daylight before I realised it was hanging by that handle, six feet above my head. The moment I saw it, those huge strips of scorched lawn came back to me in a flash. 'All my own work,' I mused as I set up the stepladder.

It's about six months since I fell off a ladder. That was from a height of about twenty feet, but because I knew I was falling I had time to sort myself out and prepare an emergency exit roll.

Twenty feet is a long time. Six feet takes you completely by surprise and leaves you no alternative but to fall as nature intended, in a painful heap.

It would have been an interesting experiment in elementary physics: A man at the top of a stepladder unexpectedly encounters a large headless bird of prey which he has mistaken for an old rag and lifted up for a closer look, he gets the fright of his life, consequently the stepladder goes in one direction and the man in the other, do they make contact with the ground simultaneously or one at a time?

I'm not sure what was worse, discovering that the rag was in fact a big dead bird or realising that there was a grisly flat red stump where its head should have been.

At least I got a closer look, because it was now lying two inches from my nose. As I rolled away I made sure I banged my head on some logs.

By this time Ian was my least favourite father-in-law and he was getting blamed for everything. My wife was not so sure.

"Do you honestly think my father bit the head off a hawk, or whatever it is, and stuck it in that thing in the pend, six or seven feet up a wall, just so you could find it and get the fright of your life?" she asked, or words to that effect.

I had to think about this. It could have been an insurance job, but more likely it was a cat. But how it got up a straight wall with a big bird in its mouth was a mystery. The stepladder was fifty yards away beside the greenhouse.

I tried to imagine which one of our regular feline visitors would be capable of committing such a heinous crime.

Was it the little grey cat who looks like he's wearing a white waistcoat, or the jet black one who seems to be smiling all the time and who loves to snake himself around my ankles purring like a distant lawnmower, or the daft ginger cat up the road who chases tractors?

One of them had graduated from stalking sparrows to decapitating a fighting fit hawk that was more than capable of defending itself.

The contraption was full of bits of that hawk so I cleaned it out and gave it to Ian without a word. My wife however, told him about the headless hawk so he didn't use the thing for about a month. Roughly the length of time it took for him to stop going 'yugh' whenever he passed it.

Over the following weeks headless birds became something of a theme in our garden.

Usually I disposed of them before anyone else jumped two feet in the air. But I'm sure our postie thinks we're into voodoo. I saw him gazing suspiciously at my National Geographic after he had almost stepped on the umpteenth headless crow.

I still find it hard to believe this is the work of an ordinary cat and I have nightmares about meeting the beast of Bodmin moor of a crisp autumn evening, its eyes green with bloodlust.

Almost as worrying is the prospect of encountering all those poor bird's heads. Cats love to secrete things and there must be at least a shoe box of them lying in wait somewhere. Which is something to look forward to. In the meantime it's another good reason for avoiding the back of the shed.

Black Ice

The only thing you really need to remember about black ice, is that it's black. Perhaps because it seems such a contradiction in terms I've always found it a particularly slippery concept to get to grips with.

You would think the onset of winter would be a clue, but obviously I must have a memory that comes in monthly instalments. Every year I have the same icy close encounter on the same stretch of winding road about half a mile from our house and vow I'll know better next time. So much for vows.

Apparently the chances of you having an accident increase the closer you get to your home. Presumably your guard starts lowering as you turn onto that road you know like the back of your hand.

I was driving up the back of that hand chatting to my wife when we seemed to enter another dimension. This is the one where your car turns into a light as a feather toboggan and thinks it can fly, a potentially lethal cross between a snowboard and Chitty, Chitty, Bang, Bang.

I loved that film when I was a kid and I loved that weird flying car. I used to dream about driving it to school. I would take all my pals with me of course and then dive bomb the bullies as we circled the playground.

Who would have believed that my dream was about to come true and turn into a nightmare.

I don't remember there being any hint of anything untoward. Every driver is connected to the road through the steering wheel and I'm normally very receptive to the slightest change in the amount of friction rolling underneath me.

Maybe I was distracted. My wife and I were laughing about something, but in an instant our smiles were wiped off our faces and transformed into wide-eyed terror. You would almost think we were asking for trouble, like a couple in a horror film who are too happy for their own good as they travel towards the nemesis the audience know is waiting for them around the next bend.

I had just left the straight section of the road and was about to take that fateful bend. I was doing about 40mph; you can only drive faster than that on this road if you're 17 and have just passed your test.

Suddenly, an invisible force seemed to grab the steering wheel and pull it sharply down to the right so that the car veered violently onto the other side of the road. As if that wasn't scary enough, the car speeded up and felt as if it had left the road altogether. For a moment I would have sworn it was flying through thin air. It was quite a trick now I look back on it, the sort of thing people pay good money for.

At the time this didn't occur to us. My wife was mainly concerned with the fact that I had taken leave of my senses, never mind the right side of the road, and had decided to kill us. Funnily enough we had recently watched a documentary about a bloke who had been convicted of killing his wife by driving them into a river and claiming it was an accident. My wife must have made a mental note about this, even though the nearest river was several miles away.

"What on earth are you doing?" she shouted, gripping onto the door with one hand and the dashboard with the other.

"I'm not doing anything!" I shouted back, as I fought with the steering wheel and tried to pull us back onto the right side of the road.

"Well do something, we're on the wrong side of the road!" screamed my wife, as if I hadn't noticed, but the car wouldn't respond.

Even though I had braked and corrected the steering wheel, to my utter amazement we were hurtling towards the bank on the other side of the road. I have no idea what lies behind this bank, a field I think, but there could have been a deep ditch and I wasn't in the mood to find out.

We were both now hanging on for our lives as the car mounted the bank, which is about two and a half metres high, and started riding along it. The world turned on its elbow and I think gravity saved us from flying over the top into the great unknown.

A hundred yards further on; the dense wood strides right down to meet the road and seems to be held in check by a stout fence. We could easily have ploughed into it, but my battle with the steering wheel and the weight of the car pulled us back onto the road and straight into a terrific spin.

My wife and I have discussed this several times, but neither of us can remember precisely how many times the car spun right round. I think it was probably twice but my wife maintains it was three times. One thing's for sure; simple arithmetic deserts you when you think you are going to die.

I actually remember thinking that our number was up and deciding that this was no way to go. We were busy, we had things to do and it was quite a nice day..

Fortunately this road is not very busy, but it does see a certain amount of farm traffic and the odd delivery van. We were just lucky that nothing was coming the other way, or I'm not sure I would be writing this column.

We must have travelled more than a hundred yards during our anti-clockwise spin and when we finally came to an abrupt bone crunching halt we were back on the right side of the road. Unfortunately we were facing oncoming traffic and the back of the car was embedded in the muddy verge.

To be honest I had closed my eyes. I hate carnival rides and I had just been on the biggest one of my life. As usual, when the world started blurring in front of me I gave up and hoped for the best.

My wife and I were both severely dazed by the experience, but the main thing was, in fact the miraculous thing was, we seemed to be unscathed.

We looked at one another gravely for a long moment and then burst out laughing, probably because we were so relieved to be alive. But then the back of the car began sinking rather worryingly so I quickly drove off and got us back onto the road facing the right way. Just as well I did because we were about to slip backwards into a deep burn.

I was convinced my car had been seriously damaged but almost unbelievably there was not a scratch on it. You would have thought it had never happened. But our little joyless ride left an indelible mark and we have both learned to expect the unexpected. In my usual cheery way I took it as a reality check, one minute you're wondering what's for tea and the next it could be lights out.

Hot and very Bothered

I hate being in small-enclosed spaces. It's not a full-blown phobia, I don't start shaking uncontrollably and break out into a sweat; I just can't wait to escape.

I use the word escape in its fullest sense, because as far as I'm concerned lifts, store rooms, cupboards and even changing rooms are all malevolent traps, that will eventually close in on me.

I like to put this down to being shut up in a cupboard when I was a kid by a teacher who obviously couldn't stand the sight of me, but it's probably just a nasty by-product of my over active imagination.

A friend asked me recently in a lift what I imagined was going to happen to me in these confined places, and I immediately reeled off a horrifying list that made his hair stand on end. From now on he says he's taking the stairs.

I also don't like being too hot, not unless I'm lying beside a pool on the Riviera. My acupuncturist told me that a hot head is a sign of too much mental activity, which of course I took as a compliment. Get off the brain train, he said, and hit the track.

He went on to explain with startling clarity even I could understand that all my energies were going straight to my head and how I had to coax some of them back down to my feet, which incidentally were in a state of constant permafrost. So I took his advice and went to the gym.

After a few weeks it began to work, I was so stiff and sore a hot head was the least of my worries, but my cold feet had completely gone, because they now throbbed like enormous boils.

Having heated myself up to a rich red glow I decided I was more than ready to sample some of the other delights on offer at the gym.

I was also intrigued by the peculiarly healthy glow my son Adam sported when he left the gym. It was an enviable contrast to my dragged through the wringer look, which unfortunately, usually stayed with me for several days afterwards.

Apparently Adam had the sauna to thank for his spruced up appearance.

"You don't have to do a thing," he said, "Just relax."

This sounded too good to be true, which it was, but at the time I couldn't wait.

It's always freezing outside the gym, a relentless icy gale scuds across the door giving everyone that arctic explorer look. So I reckoned the sauna would be just the thing to warm my cockles. This was before I realised that 'sauna' was Finnish for the combined forces of my two worst nightmares.

As I worked myself up into a lather on the rowing machine I imagined the well-appointed cosiness of the sauna. There was bound to be a bevy of blond Scandinavian women serving ice cold drinks, or at least there was the last time I saw a sauna. Admittedly it was occupied at the time by James Bond and a clutch of Russian double agents.

The excitement was now killing me, but it was nothing compared to the effect the sauna would have.

Apparently it's not a good idea to work out in a gym and then dash into the nearest sauna. I read this on the way out.

I couldn't read it on the way in because I was so fascinated by the sight of complete strangers, of all sexes I should add, casually strolling around in nothing but loosely knotted towels. If the fire alarm went off we were all down for double pneumonia.

Little did I realise the sauna was in fact where they rehearsed the fire.

There were several rooms to choose from, and not wishing to rush into things; I examined all of them by peering in through the little window in the doors.

In the biggest room, a young woman who was sitting chatting to an elderly couple, almost jumped out of her towel with fright when she saw my face staring in at her through the steam, or Löyly as the Finns would say. So that ruled that one out.

Adam diplomatically steered me away, suggesting it might be an idea if we try a cooler room first and work our way up to the hottest, and I agreed.

Clutching our towels we scurried back to the first set of rooms passing a trio of middle-aged ladies discussing their arrangements for Christmas dinner, one of them was having a curry. For a moment I thought I recognised them, but bereft of their clothes it was difficult to tell. I thought it best not to say anything, since I had already been marked down as a Peeping Tom.

With some deliberation Adam selected a room and in we went. I'm not sure what I expected, probably something larger than my shed, but I thought it all just stopped a little too abruptly.

There were no sunloungers either, or waitresses, which was just as well because there wasn't room to stir a Martini.

"Is it standing room only?" I asked, but Adam had already clambered up onto what I would call a high shelf.

"It's not a shelf," said Adam giving me a hand up, "it's a Lauteet."

And there we perched on our Lauteet, precariously scrunched up like a couple of huge ornaments with our heads hard up against the ceiling waiting for nothing to happen. I couldn't have been more uncomfortable if I had been bundled into a suitcase.

The Finns have been doing this at around 100 degrees centigrade for a thousand years so they must have a lot of spare time on their hands.

A few moments later two enormous bald men who had apparently over imbibed the previous night joined us. One of them told the other that he had been off his face. Judging by the look of him he had put it back on in the dark.

The moment our little box filled up with flesh the heat suddenly struck me and I remembered how much I hated being cooked in my own sweat in a tiny box. The air was now so hot it was burning the lining off the inside of my nose and the big men were getting bigger by the second as they slowly melted towards me.

Adam meanwhile seemed totally unaffected by the experience; in fact he looked particularly chuffed with himself. When one of the blokes broke wind I decided I didn't want my impurities drained out of me. I had spent years accumulating them and sometimes I think they're the only things that keep me together.

As I stumbled out shaking and sweating my head rattled like a gigantic cinder. I had never been so hot in my life. I was fairly certain my hair was on fire and the soles of my feet felt as if they had been cooked to a crisp.

I was only in the sauna for about three minutes and I can't remember how much it cost me, but it was worth every penny just for the privilege of being reminded that I'm not oven ready.

The Party Pooper

An old friend whom I haven't seen for some time told me I was a party pooper recently. Which, I have to say, came as a bit of a surprise.

I wouldn't have minded if we were in the middle of a huge wild ceilidh and I was doing my wallflower act, but I was reviewing a relatively serious play. All I wanted to do was sit in my usual seat but apparently if I did then the play's big special effect would be ruined for me.

I weighed up the benefits and promptly sat in my favourite seat. In a theatre, leg room is more important than special effects.

But I was haunted and puzzled by the remark and I carried it away with me like an itch.

Wrestling with the incident later I just couldn't work out how my friend had come to this conclusion. I hadn't seen or spoken to her for years but she was absolutely certain that I was marked down as a wet blanket.

Either it was a spur of the moment thing because she caught me being stupidly stubborn, or I'm the last resort on everyone's party list. The trouble is both are true so I'm none the wiser.

This is of course the perfect time to test out my new-found status because this is the party-pooper season. With so many organised events of premeditated revelry to choose from it's hard to keep a respectably low profile without turning yourself into Billy No-Mates for the rest of the year. You really have to keep your wits about you or you never know what you'll get up to. The road to hell is paved with inattention.

Last Christmas while our office party was in full swing I successfully slipped away just minutes before all my colleagues, young and not so sprightly, were encouraged up onto the restaurant tables and started dancing with alarming abandon.

Being naturally suspicious I wondered why the staff were removing all the candles, and then the empty glasses and anything vaguely breakable. The music was getting louder and I smiled to myself thinking, 'Uh oh, here we go it's tabletop dancing time'.

It was about three-thirty in the afternoon. Outside, it was beginning to get dark, it was snowing lightly and the streets were busy with crazy-eyed shoppers. I made some feeble excuse about not feeling well, which in fact was partly true and vanished into the crowds.

I don't think anyone was bothered and most barely noticed, but in true party-pooper style I breathed a big sigh of relief and reckoned I had made a lucky and timely escape.

How right I was. As I drove past the restaurant I could clearly see my friends strutting their stuff, rather dangerously I thought on top of the tables. The passengers in the bus in front of me must have got a real eye-full.

I was told later that the restaurant blinds had to be closed because a crowd of young men had gathered to leer at all the young ladies in our office blithely disporting themselves.

In a way I suppose I couldn't come to terms with the fact that just a few hours earlier we were all working away totally involved in our various activities and then by the middle of the afternoon, as if by magic, everyone was unleashed. Personally I've never thought it a good idea to dance on a full stomach.

"Sounds like great fun!" enthused my wife, until I told her I had done a runner.

"Oh dear," she tutted, "You really must learn to let yourself go."

The trouble is, I don't think I have anything left to let go anymore. It was all let go years ago. I'm out there all the time, giving it large as they say, on a weekly basis.

When I tell people I'm regularly surrounded by hordes of wild women dancing and screaming they can't believe my luck. But when I tell them it's all in a night's work and I get paid for it they still can't believe my luck.

There is a difference of course between sitting in a theatre writing a review of a big hot driving show that has everyone dancing in the aisles and going loudly berserk, namely, I haven't paid for the privilege.

But somehow all that unleashed elation must rub off, because I often come home completely exhausted and high as a kite.

"My, you've certainly had a good time." My wife will say when I stagger in foaming at the mouth after yet another thundering ride on the groove train.

If I have had a whale of a time then it must be by proxy, or osmosis.

The downside is that fifteen years of this sort of thing on a regular basis has made me lazy when it comes to actually letting myself go. Why bother I think, when other people will do it for me at their expense.

This means I'm not even the bridesmaid, never mind the groom, I'm the witness. Sometimes however I do feel like a square old teacher chaperoning a school dance.

One sure-fire way around this I've discovered is to take my wife with me. She was my secret weapon recently against my inertia at a Gospel choir concert, and it worked like a charm. The first time the audience rose to their feet clapping it was only fifteen minutes into the show and I had just started writing my review so I sat barricaded by a stockade of bobbing bodies.

The next time, my wife reminded me that I had come to enjoy myself by pulling me up onto my feet by the ear. I felt much better. Across the aisles there were two old ladies getting down and funky to the soulfood beat and earlier they had made me feel like that square old teacher's crusty great grandfather.

I can't say that I actually danced of my own volition but I was cajoled into dancing by the force of the crowd. Bending like the proverbial reed was easier than suffering bodily harm. I even found clapping along out of time to the music highly therapeutic. By the end of the night I was ready to get up on anyone's table and dare them to call me a party-pooper.

Last week at our office party we were back in the same restaurant and I was revving up nicely. I had a few cool moves up my sleeve gleaned from the Gospel choir. I was going to prove to everyone that I wasn't the type of bloke who danced like his father.

But the fates conspired against me. Just as I was slipping into my dancing shoes a phone call summoned me to finish some urgent business.

"A likely story." Said my wife despairingly. But it was true. I left that restaurant and my jovial pals on a cliffhanger of uncertainty, never knowing how big a prat I would have made of myself.

On the other hand it was the perfect party-poopers getaway. In fact you'd almost think I had arranged it. As if.

One Singer, One Song

During the festive season if you happen to be giving your all in a Karaoke club - standing by your man like a big spending bat out of hell with the wind beneath your wings, and you spot a bloke squashed against the bar doing a Victor Meldrew impression, screaming, "I don't believe it!" at the top of his voice, that's me.

It's a cruel fact of the Karaoke world that Karaoke singers require an audience other than themselves. As a fully-fledged Karaoke audience member I know what it's like to have your favourite songs tortured beyond recognition before your very eyes.

As a form of entertainment Karaoke owes more to the arena of ancient Rome than it does to the traditional culture of Japan, which to be fair has always encouraged singalongs as a form of ritual punishment.

However, there is something decidedly Roman about watching your wife and her boss crooning "I got you Babe" into one another's alcohol diffused eyes while a crowd of complete strangers chants the rude version of the chorus.

Since I'm normally the sober as a judge chauffeur on these occasions, this is when I slip into my Victor Meldrew mode and pray that I'm teleported to a planet where the microphone is a thing of the future.

I could think of far worse ways for people to make a fool of themselves but it might take me some time. This of course is the secret of Karaoke's success, as a medium for embarrassing people it is unsurpassed.

Karaoke was born in the urban Japanese city of Kobe thirty years ago, but it stewed in the eastern mindset for at least two decades before it escaped to infiltrate the western world and become the choice of weapon preferred by nine out of ten Sadistic exhibitionists, and consequently a 13 billion dollar industry. You can even annoy your friends in cyberspace by joining a Karaoke community on the Internet.

The word "Karaoke" is derived from two Japanese words strung together. "Kara" from "karappo," means empty, while "Oke" has been shortened from "okesutura," meaning orchestra. So, Karaoke actually means 'empty orchestra'. It's a pity it didn't mean 'empty bar'.

Every time I'm faced with my wife or a friend doing their Stars in Their Eyes routine I remember the first time I encountered the Karaoke menace.

It was about ten years ago and appropriately enough it was a Hogmanay party. Ever since I was a boy, the words, "One singer, one song," have sent me running for cover amongst the dirty dishes in the kitchen.

But when Andy our party host brought home his Karaoke machine from his pub I was none the wiser, in fact none of us were. We were told it was a sort of jukebox and promised a good laugh. The dull looking machine however, sat in a corner of the room largely ignored by everyone.

It was a small black box, which appeared to be impersonating what I would have called a practice amplifier, the sort of thing teenagers with electric instruments keep in their bedroom to ward off the ageing process.

Assisted by the excesses of alcohol this harmless looking box remained something of a mystery. We all agreed it was probably an amplifier, but none of us could work out what it was meant to amplify.

Even Andy who had bought the thing wasn't sure how to work it, but he was happy to shrug us off and fall backwards into the comfort of his favourite armchair. Apparently he had fulfilled his part of the bargain by bringing the machine home in the first place and now he was peeved because everyone wanted him to be a scientist.

Since this was obviously a technical problem all the blokes felt compelled to carry out a personal inspection on the mute device. This involved solemnly fiddling with its knob, knowingly pressing a few buttons, turning it upside down and then shaking it like a rattle. One genius even plugged it in, but all to no effect. So it was left it for dead. It was of course the women it was waiting for.

By two in the morning you would have thought it might have given up, but this if often when the Karaoke bug can be at its most lethal. This is also of course when all the introverts have forgotten about it.

While I was at the front door greeting a group of reasonably dishevelled late arrivals I heard my wife singing "Start spreading the news..." at the top of her voice.

It was so loud it sounded as if she was out in the street canvassing for votes from one of those political party vans, but some of the newcomers knew exactly what was going on and before they had their coats off they were heading straight for it shouting, "Karaoke!"

And that was the start of it. I followed everyone into the living room where my wife was doing her Liza Minnelli impression and all I could think was, who on earth gave her a microphone and how does she suddenly know all the words.

Andy was now looking very pleased with himself as he lounged back in his chair like a talent scout whose protégé has just broken into the top ten.

Andy of course was at last enjoying a return on his investment and he could already see the potential rise in his bar trade. To me it was still a menacing black box, but to my wife it was a captive audience with the possibility of a hit single, a five-album deal and a world tour.

Funnily enough it didn't work out like that. In that dark age before computerisation Karaoke singers had to rely on a pack of cards for their lyrics. Even if you're stone cold sober it's difficult to sing into a microphone while juggling a handful of lyrics. The result was inevitably musical mayhem.

This is when the true horror of Karaoke struck home, because the people it infected couldn't have cared less what was being sung. While my wife belted out the words to 'River Deep Mountain High' the machine churned out the music for 'The White Cliffs of Dover'. Geographically speaking I suppose she was on the right track.

Since that first fateful encounter I've been Victor Meldrew to my wife's Tina Turner, Judy Garland, and Barbra Streisand. Only once in a Karaoke bar in Spain was she lost for words. It was more of a corridor than a bar, along which potential pop stars formed an orderly queue.

It was only when we managed to muscle our way into within earshot of the proceedings that my wife's enthusiasm thawed and vanished. What we had assumed was a recording turned out to be a tiny teenager from Wolverhampton with a voice like a rock angel. One after another the amateur performers took the stage and sang with such astonishing power that our jaws couldn't drop any further.

"That's not real Karaoke." Declared my wife as we strode off down the starlit boulevard. "Those people could really sing."

Those Who Wait Also Serve

If you often find yourself short of chatty company you might like to consider taking a seat at your local outpatients waiting room. I'm not suggesting you waste valuable NHS time and if you're worried about occupying a chair under false pretences you could take your own one along.

One of those fold-up jobs that fishermen and artists use would probably do very nicely. A flask of coffee and some sandwiches would also come in handy, although you can always buy some from the WRVS trolleys.

You don't even need to be ill; in fact it's probably better if you're not. The last thing sick folk want are other sick folk nattering on about their complaints, so go armed with a collection of funny anecdotes. If you get stuck remember there's always plenty of Reader's Digests lying around and laughter really is the best medicine.

If you're of a cheerful disposition you will be rewarded with a living soap opera you can take home with you and cherish always. After an hour or two in a waiting room people are usually desperate to open up and share the most intimate details of their family lives.

If you've done a bit of counselling then all the better, but no professional training or qualifications are necessary.

Once you've got yourself into the waiting room – you could always say you've come to collect someone, it is absolutely vital that you sit amongst a group of women. If you've no other choice one woman will do, but she might just turn out to be the biggest bore in the place. So take your time before you sit down and weigh up the options.

Whatever you do never sit next to a man, because they'll just read the magazines and you won't get a word out of them and you might as well be at home.

You might also like to consider choosing an outpatients where you won't catch anything, like an Eye clinic for instance. I'm speaking of course from recent experience.

We were half an hour early for my mother-in-law's appointment at the Eye clinic. Which doesn't mean anything in NHS terms except that we had half an hour longer to wait.

Isabelle has had acute Glaucoma, a condition common amongst Eskimos and people of African origin, so as you can imagine there's been some rummaging around in the roots of the family tree. But with little success. Consequently Isabelle still refuses to answer to Eskimo Nell.

Having said that it was cold enough outside the Eye clinic to warrant it - minus six to be precise. And it wasn't much warmer inside, something to do with the concrete floors I imagine.

I left my wife in charge of the waiting and went off to conduct some business, the son-in-law's prerogative. Isabelle was only in for a check up so I reckoned that an hour would do it at the most, but I had forgotten to set my watch to hospital time.

The Eye clinic is just one of dozens of satellite buildings that swarm around inside a huge hospital complex specially designed to deter you from ever finding them. On my return I discovered it completely by accident because I saw my wife standing outside the door.

"Brilliantly timed." I said to myself. My wife was obviously on the lookout for me and here I was ready to take everyone home. It was still minus six degrees so I thought my wife was being particularly vigilant. In fact she had just nipped out for a breather.

Isabelle still hadn't been seen, but she had at least moved from the waiting room to the queue in the corridor. However, they had now listened to so many sensational life stories that my wife's head was spinning.

"It's like Coronation Street in there," said my wife, "Except without the ad breaks."

"It couldn't be that good." I said, so my wife brought me up to speed on the various storylines so far and they were so complex I almost lost the plot.

"So the first lady's grandson is not really her grandson and his mother is his auntie who lives in Australia but he doesn't know this. The second lady's niece has run away with a chef from Paisley who won ten grand on Who Wants To Be a Millionaire and the third lady's husband is in prison for burgling his own house." I repeated tentatively.

"No, no, no..." corrected my wife, "The first lady's grandson is a chef and his auntie who is his real mother won the ten grand, the other lady..."

Baffled and freezing I just wanted to get inside the clinic. My feet were so cold they had forgotten they were feet.

Seated in a line along the consulting room corridor were all the characters in this living soap opera. I was introduced to them and settled back for the next instalment.

When Isabelle was eventually called, my wife accompanied her and left me to follow the extraordinary life story of lady number one. She was a lovely woman and remarkably cheerful considering the trials she had experienced.

As her story unfolded in candid detail I was completely gripped. I only wished I could have reciprocated but compared to her daily family dramas I'd had a very tame time of it.

For almost an hour and a half I sat in that corridor enthralled by the company of complete strangers. It was a bit like listening to a radio play, but with the added advantage of being able to ask questions.

When my wife and her Mum finally appeared I was sorry to leave in case I missed something. But then we had to go to the hospital pharmacy and pick up Isabelle's prescription. The receptionist warned that we might have to wait some time, so I volunteered without hesitation, much to my wife's amazement. Isabelle on the other hand thought I was a fine upstanding son-in-law.

We had to drive to the pharmacy, which was on the other side of the hospital, in the basement. I took one of those huge lifts that opens at both ends and for one creepy moment as we sank downward I didn't think the doors were going to shut.

I had been told to follow the thin red line so I did and after passing row upon row of filed x-rays – at least a dozen of which must have been mine, I ended up half a mile later almost back outside the door to the Eye clinic. At one point I passed a group of people queuing like tightrope walkers on the red line, which I thought was taking instructions a bit far.

After making several wrong detours I finally struck gold. The pharmacy had a little waiting room full of elderly women. "Do you come here often?" I asked as I sat down in the middle of them.

When I eventually made it back to the car an hour later my wife and her Mum thought I'd been abducted. However, it was worth the wait because the stories I had to tell...

The Strange Flower

I decided that I had to buy some orchids. There was no longer any doubt in my mind. It was as if I had been brainwashed, very slowly, over a period of about six months I reckon, but now I was ready to take the plunge.

As a rule exotic flowering houseplants hold little interest for me. I prefer the big green jungle look of the cast iron Aspidistra. But last year, completely by chance, I walked into an orchid exhibition at the Kelvingrove Botanical Gardens in Glasgow and I've been discreetly haunted by orchids ever since.

At the time I was amazed and delighted by these strange plants with their surreal flowers straight out of Japanese woodcut prints.

Encountering them in the flesh was a different matter. To me they looked as if they had been sent from another planet. At first glance the highly complex blooms appeared impossibly frail yet they were heavy and firm to the touch, like a succulent.

Some of the plants were growing from the trunks of trees and the green spikes with their tiny ball joints looked more like insects with fantastic heads, mouths gaping wide to catch anything that flew past.

The sheer variety of design and colour kept me moving from one to the next. The fact that some produced a scent powerful enough to make my head spin while others remained mutely sterile fascinated me. I dodged around the exhibition sniffing anything that didn't move like a daft dog and when I found one that was particularly powerful I made sure everyone savoured it.

As we moved from the orchid exhibition into the carnivorous plant house it occurred to me how little difference there actually was between animal and plant life. Suddenly The Day of Triffids didn't seem so far fetched.

I forgot about the orchids until recently when I read the HG Wells short story The Flowering of the Strange Orchid in which an enthusiast is almost assassinated by a rare specimen and the flower attained an air of mystique that worked on me like a charm.

I then began encountering them everywhere. People I had always assumed couldn't have grown a boil had beautiful orchids.

It was as if I was being stalked, and for a time I was genuinely scared I was going to become a member of a nutty flower-worshipping club. I've always been suspicious of anyone with a singular obsession. But then in one way or another I suppose we're all trainspotters.

In any case, most of the orchid owners I had met didn't know the first thing about them, apart from the fact that they liked the look of them. I had also been assured that growing orchids was no longer a blend of intense labour and horticultural science.

So that was it, my mind was made up; I even knew just the place to buy my orchids. I remembered seeing them for sale at our local Botanical Gardens and by sheer coincidence it was the very place my wife wanted to visit.

If I hadn't been driving I would have been rubbing my hands all the way there. Unfortunately my career as an orchid expert was to be short lived.

It had completely slipped my mind to mention the orchids to my wife, probably because she would have looked at me in exactly the way she looked at me when I steered her into the Gardens' shop and told her I was buying orchids.

Actually it was more of a little laugh than a look, but it spoke volumes.

"Why would you suddenly want to buy orchids?" she asked. It was a good question, which I couldn't really answer, short of saying that it was just something I had been thinking about.

My wife advised me to keep thinking about it until it went away. She had the same problem with all manner of things and it worked for her.

But the orchids were right in front of me and they were even more extraordinary than I had imagined. There were several types in bloom, nothing too exotic, mostly whites and creams.

My wife squinted at them and pronounced them all a bit far fetched. Which was exactly my point. The fact that you could live with something so curious seemed almost illicit.

"You realise you'll have to look after it yourself?" declared my wife, and I nodded like a little boy in a pet shop about to become the proud owner of his first puppy.

There was however a large matter of the price. You can tell something is expensive when even I'm forced to say "How much?"

For a moment I hoped I was reading the price wrong, but no such luck. My wife could see I was downcast so she tried to palm me off with a cactus, but I had already forgotten about the orchids and moved on. Up on a shelf against the far wall I had spotted something even stranger, an absolutely enormous salmon pink flower growing impossibly from the top of a single thick green stalk about two feet high.

Just to add to the spectacle the bulb was as big as a grapefruit and it was jammed inside a pot that was so small it looked like a prime case of plant cruelty.

This was better than any old orchid and it was a quarter of the price. After much debate my wife convinced me to buy one that wasn't in flower, it also had two stalks, a giant one and a baby brother that had just pierced its way through the dome of the big bulb.

"A lovely Amaryllis," announced the bloke at the till, "A good choice." I told him about the orchids and how they were too expensive and to my amazement he agreed, then he warned me to do my homework about the Amaryllis.

"Excellent," I thought, "A weird flowering plant and homework!"

I had that club joining feeling again, but I kept it to myself. We went to the supermarket while the Amaryllis waited in the car.

Two hours later back at the house the plant looked very different from the one I had bought. For a start it was no longer gravity defying. When I lifted it out of its polythene container the stalk flopped around like a limp dead grass snake.

"I see you've gone for the shortcut and killed it on the way home." Remarked my wife.

Ever hopeful I stood the floppy plant near a radiator and mounted a constant pot-side vigil. Within ten minutes the stalk

85

began to move and slowly writhe, convinced it was back home in the Peruvian Andes the snake was coming back to life.

I carefully carried it to my study where it is now proudly displayed, like a big green spear waiting to be fired at unwelcome intruders. For a plant named after a shepherdess from Greek mythology it has a decidedly fierce aspect.

"But when it flowers it will be the Danny La Rue of plants." Observed my wife. Apparently I'll be lucky if the flower lasts a week. I feel a singular obsession coming on.

Room 101

My wife's been having a recurring nightmare. It's about a room she can never find in a huge ever-changing building and of course she's late and weighed down like a packhorse with heavy arm-stretching cases. Even worse, she's awake at the time.

I knew something was up when I asked her where she wanted dropped off one morning as we reached the huge building and she changed her mind seven times within two hundred yards.

I can understand her indecision; you can drive right round this place, and find an entrance at every turn. It's a college of further education, so it likes to present an open door no matter where you're coming from.

"See that room there?" asked my wife edgily, pointing to a classroom on the ground floor, "Which entrance would you go through to reach that room?"

My wife knows I have some experience of this college, but thinking this was a trick question I decided that any entrance would do, but I was wrong.

"Never mind, I'll find it if it kills me!" she said brusquely then strode off. Actually it was more of a lilting hobble because she had forgotten to distribute the weight of her cases. Livingston probably took less with him into the African interior.

The similarity it seems is not so far fetched.

Unbeknown to me my wife had been fearlessly tracking this illusive room for many weeks, with lessening success. Ironically the exterior wall of the room is just a short walk from one of the college gates. You can actually see inside the room from the pavement.

When my wife walks past it she can see her friends through the windows, chatting animatedly, almost smugly she imagines because they've found the room without having a nervous breakdown. In fact they haven't even broken out into a sweat, never mind a blind panicking run.

It's normally still dark at this time of the morning, and the room's comforting lights tease her with the promise of brighter things to come. Her friends wave tantalisingly to her, and if she is slightly late they tap their watches and mouth "Hurry up!"

When she didn't know any better she used to shout back "I'll see you in a minute!" But now she screams, "Help, Let me in!"

One desperate morning she even considered asking me to park under one of the windows so she could climb up onto the car roof and be dragged inside by her pals. I told her that might be all right for a one-off emergency, but on a regular basis she would have to bring a stepladder

The trouble is, once my wife gets inside the college the room plays an expert game of hide and seek with her. But she reckons its cheating. Either it moves constantly ahead of her, or it's able to blend itself like a chameleon into its surroundings, until it almost disappears. She has a sneaking suspicion that she passes it without realising it.

She says it's the only room she has ever known that you have to go upstairs to get down to. This doesn't seem that unreasonable to me. The college is really two buildings joined by an overhead bridge. Ironically if my wife was in her car she would find the room in minutes, but her sense of direction seems to rely on having a steering wheel in front of her.

I offered to buy one for her, but she thought the compass was bad enough – I had told her that the room lies in the South West side of the college.

This sounds too much like quantum physics to my wife so she resorts to the tried and tested method of keeping a sharp lookout for anyone she thinks might be heading for the same room and sticks to them like a human limpet. One morning after wondering around the college for half an hour she followed a set of complete strangers and ended up in the canteen.

By sheer chance a group of her friends were on their tea break so she pleaded with them to take her back to the room with them. "Don't leave me here!" She whimpered like the shipwrecked Ben Gunn.

I've been in this college many times and it's constantly being upgraded so corridors and staircases can be blocked off when you least expect it, in fact they can disappear altogether only to reappear weeks later in a completely different place. My wife believes all this constant upheaval has had a harmful effect on the building's Karma.

"It's disorientated," she reasons, "And if it doesn't know where it's going how does it expect me to work it out?"

She has come very close on several occasions to cracking this maze but then the college embarks on a major restructuring programme and she's back where she started - asking people for directions which at the time sound perfectly understandable but which seconds later turn into Lithuanian.

Even worse were the smart alecks who informed her there were at least five ways to reach the room, and then asked which one she would like. Faced with the prospect of multiple choice she ran off in the first direction that was agreeably decorated and began taking lifts that led right back to the entrance she had just come in.

Since the start of a new term she has discovered she is not alone. Along every corridor equally frantic people fly past. Sometimes one of them will stop and offer to pay my wife to take them to their designated room. Needless to say she always knows exactly how to get to their room and they know how to get to hers. My wife can't understand why they can't all just swap rooms.

One morning last week she found the room completely by chance. She turned a corner and there it was with its door open, waiting to welcome her. Since she had allowed herself the usual half an hour frantic searching time she was far too early.

This meant she could spend some time pacing around the empty room fretting in case she had got her timetable wrong, and debating about whether to go to the office, only to discover she was right in the first place and unable to find her way back.

There is a college map of course, which is available from the office, but my wife can't find the office two days in a row. I keep telling her it's near the main entrance, and she just keeps asking which main entrance? Knowing her luck the maps are probably issued from the room next door to the room she can't find.

The room also acts as a Bermuda Triangle, or rather Rectangle, because people who use it keep disappearing. Every week my wife's class gets smaller and she suspects everyone is moving gradually to another room that's easier to find. Eventually she'll be on her own with no one to wave out the window at but passing pedestrians, all hurrying on their way to their very own versions of Room 101.

A Load of Rubbish

My wife's idea of a country stroll is everyone else's idea of a drive, particularly if she's in power walking mode. To achieve this you have to firmly clench your buttocks together and take the smallest steps you can humanly manage without tying your ankles in knots. Meanwhile the top half of your body has to look as if it's running. For some reason I can only do this when no one is looking.

The moment I catch sight of a fellow rambler or dog walker I'm back slouching with the worst of them, pointing out imaginary landmarks of interest. Meanwhile my wife is on the distant horizon and I have to sprint through her vapour trail to catch her up.

When I was many stones heavier this would have been almost impossible because I would have been running uphill and down dale and fording streams like St Christopher with an 8 year old child on my back – I worked it out.

Now I travel solo there is less chance of me keeling over, although the temptation to buckle is still hard to resist. Unfortunately if I stopped for any reasonable length of time it wouldn't be long before my wife reported me as a missing person.

My father had the right idea - a walk in the country was something you did in order to reach a reasonably comfortable seat from which you could marvel at the wonders of nature. This worked very well because he always got the comfortable seat.

Even now I have a talent for picking the sharpest, dampest rock, or the only anthill within ten miles on which to park my weary fragile end.

I always think a little home comforts wouldn't go amiss on these jaunts. I'm not asking for several square metres of shagpile and a remote control, a simple stool would probably do the job.

You can imagine my delight last weekend when I discovered an extremely generous anonymous benefactor had come to my aid.

We were several miles from our house and as usual I was lagging behind. Just as my feet were starting to turn to lead my wife stopped dead in her tracks. The last time she did this – to watch a family of deer lope across a field, I fell over and had a quick power nap. But this time she was laughing.

" I see you've sent the servants ahead today." She shouted, pointing in front of her, like a scout on a hunting party.

Baffled, I eventually caught up with her and saw to my delight what looked like a three-piece suite sitting on the left side of the verge, probably about thirty yards or so up the road. It was obviously waiting patiently for my custom. I couldn't believe my luck.

"Where on earth did that come from?" asked my wife.

"Who cares," I said, "I'm having a seat."

I am reliably informed it was made of green velour. Not a fabric I'm over familiar with, and that it was at least twenty years old, which meant it was probably highly inflammable.

I shrugged my shoulders.

"If it catches fire we can shove it in the burn." I declared, falling into the gentle embrace of probably the most comfortable sofa I have ever found sitting by the roadside.

The strange thing was it hadn't just been casually left in a heap. A great deal of care had been taken to lay it out. From the sofa you were afforded a perfect view through a gap in the Beech trees right across the fields to the grand Georgian house in the distance.

The two armchairs looked a little worse for wear, lovingly used I imagined, but they had been thoughtfully arranged so the whole family could relax together in front of the invisible telly that was sitting in the middle of the road. All we needed was a coffee table and a few footstools.

If it had been high summer the suite would have been even more delightful - resting on a bed of wild Ransom, and decoratively framed by the creeping Honeysuckle. Sheltered by the generous canopy of an ancient Sycamore it would have made a magical fairy bower. A sight fit to inspire any country poet.

Just as well it was green velour, black leather would have been too ostentatious and probably frightened the nervous cows.

Frankly I was in my element but my wife refused to join me. Instead she kept stalking round the suite with her fists on her hips, muttering that it was at least a comfortable van load.

For a moment I thought she was considering taking the suite home, but I think she was just trying to work out how she could return it to its rightful owner.

"I don't think it's escaped or been stolen," I said, "I reckon it's been left here intentionally."

The evidence after all was overwhelming. For a start it was very close to a popular moorland nature reserve so it would come in very handy. When the school parties arrived in the spring the children could sit on it to write up their reports or do their sketches.

There was also the not inconsiderable matter of the recycling centre which lay less than two miles away. It was open seven days a week until about eight in the evening and there was no membership fee as far as I was aware.

The owners of the suite could easily have driven there. They couldn't miss it. All they had to do was follow the trail of abandoned fridges, broken wardrobes, rolled up rotting carpets and burst bags of garden refuse which led straight to its gate.

Once inside the centre the large bloke that runs the place would have eyed them disinterestedly as they struggled with all their might to heave their sofa and chairs into a skip. But at the very last minute, just as the sofa tumbled in, he would have undoubtedly offered them a hand.

But no one would ever have seen the suite again. The owners obviously wanted the world and his wife to enjoy their favourite bit of upholstery. It had served them well and they wanted to pass it on like a treasured family heirloom for future generations of country walkers to savour. They had made a grand public gesture that no one could ignore, and it was miles better than a bench.

I felt the urge to write and thank them so I gingerly slipped a hand down the side of the sofa and grasped what I hoped was an old telephone or electricity bill, but it turned out to be a pizza take-away menu. Which on close inspection looked very tempting. If I'd had a mobile phone with me I might have placed an order.

My wife meanwhile was crossing the horizon, but I could swear I could still hear her muttering something about a van.

In the end I was glad we decided not to take the suite home. It would have been like picking wild flowers I thought, so we left it for everyone to enjoy.

Food Glorious Food

Up until a few weeks ago I knew every inch of our local supermarket but it's now turned into a gigantic aircraft hanger housing the entire stocks of the feed world campaign. There's certainly enough to go round. Admittedly not all of it was on the shelves at nine thirty in the evening when I was wandering around like a lost soul. A lot of it was standing smugly out of reach in huge wheelie cages – ordered extra large presumably to block the extra large aisles.

In one of these cages there was enough coffee to keep the population of the whole country awake for a fortnight. On another, several thousand tins of prunes would have fulfilled the same end.

Who's hungry enough around our way to eat all this stuff I have no idea, but I don't fancy their shopping bill.

Apparently the jumbo-sized supermarket is the shape of things to come but since the booze section is right at the far end it now means I have to walk a quarter of a mile from the entrance just to buy a bottle of wine. On the way I have to cross several climate zones, ranging from arctic to sub-tropical depending on how close I can get to the bakery.

I've also got to thread my way slowly through stacks of fluffy towels and scented candles and rows of clothes people will only ever wear abroad on holiday, before I even catch sight of the wine section.

Which incidentally is now the same size as the old supermarket. So there are some compensations. Ingeniously I can also see it from a considerable distance away, so the object of my desire is always tantalisingly in view. But why such frustration would suddenly inspire me to buy a fluffy towel is beyond me.

My wife assures me this is just basic modern retail psychology and not idle malice on the management's part. But the supermarket now reminds me of the type of shops you wander round in airports when your flight is delayed.

Sometimes it's hard to resist buying junk that you know you will have to ruin by cramming it into your already bulging hand luggage. There should be a scheme so you can hire fake purchases that you could stroll around with and then hand in when your flight is called.

The same money saving scheme could be applied to supermarkets. My wife and I have put a ban on food shopping before meals and have successfully cut our weekly bill by a considerable amount.

But it could be cut even further if we could hire items to fill our trolleys – we have one each for comfort, and then give the stuff back at the checkout. This would satisfy the primitive urge to over-harvest.

I pitched my surrogate product idea to one of the managers and for a moment I thought I could see her mentally crunching the numbers and the potential profits, but actually I think she was trying to figure how quickly and quietly she could get me out of her store.

Supermarkets always have their share of nutters and I wasn't about to become one of them. So when I saw her tentatively fiddling with her walkie-talkie I turned to more serious matters and asked if she had ever thought of introducing a crèche for lost husbands and she seemed to be more comfortable with this and said she would give it some thought.

The trouble is, for me supermarket shopping is a necessary evil, but for my wife it's a form of recreation and faced with the vastness of our new improved family-sized supermarket it struck me that her playground had just got ten times bigger and considerably more fascinating.

When we go our separate ways and my wife says she'll see me in a few minutes I never really believe that she means a few hours. So I go off and shop briskly and efficiently. Meanwhile my wife has been sucked into the black hole of merchandise and fired out light years away on the far side of convenience shopping.

This is a place I wouldn't even know how to begin to find, although I've tried countless methods. Zig-zagging through the store, painstakingly checking down every aisle, methodically covering every inch from one end to the other, and finally as a last resort cruising up and down the centre aisle until I've attached a posse of security guards to my tail.

But I just end up feeling completely useless because apparently I can't spot my own wife in a meagre crowd of strangers. I also feel slightly guilty, because she could have been kidnapped while I was rooting around for my favourite, nothing-else-will-do packet of crackers.

In my most desperate hours I have even started wondering if she's having an affair with one of the managers. Needles to say she laughed when I told her this, but you can't help being suspicious when someone shops for an hour and a half and only manages to put four items in their trolley.

When I'm wandering around the supermarket in search of my wife I always start fondly remembering the shops I went to as a little boy with my Mum where smiling people in aprons wrapped everything up in brown paper.

The downside of these charming reveries are the stark memories I have of being lost and searching apparently without hope for my mother. Eventually I would begin imagining what life would be like in the orphanage and then I would start conjuring up my adoptive parents who would of course be very rich and very nice to me because my Mother lost me in a shop.

Meanwhile somewhere on the other side of the huge supermarket my wife is frantically searching for me. Mobile phones are probably the answer. Instead we do what everyone else down when they are at sea in a place full of food; we start buying stuff we would never dream of eating under normal circumstances.

This of course is what the supermarket thrives on. They want us to get lost in the enchanted forest of food and fluffy towels and mindlessly fill our trolleys to the brim.

I've shopped for so long in this haphazard, accidental way that I was convinced it was normal. Until recently when we took my wife's parents down to their cosy local supermarket to do their weekly shop and learned a valuable lesson.

Even allowing for my wife's usual Houdini-like mystery tour round the aisles I seriously considered bringing a thick book with me, because my parents-in-law haven't broken any land speed records lately. But after just 20 minutes they had finished their shopping, paid for it and were ready to pack it in the car.

My father-in-law Ian stared in amazement at the two lonely loaves of bread lying at the bottom of our trolley. "Always go forward," he advised shaking his head, "Don't separate, and never give in to temptation."

I assumed he was talking about shopping and would have asked my wife's opinion if I could have found her.

Fenced In

For the past 18 months I've been having a running battle with my old larch lap fence, or at least what's left of it.

Since it looked as if it was about to blow away any minute I replaced it with the help of my neighbour Trevor, who rather magnanimously I thought at the time, let me keep all 170 square metres of it.

"No honestly you have it." He kept persisting as I tried to persuade him to take at least half. But he wouldn't hear of it and helped me carry it into our courtyard and stack it against the wall in the pend, the archway that divides our steading. There the wind would dry it out and turn it into perfect firewood and kindling for our stove.

What a guy I thought, but Trevor knew what he was doing, because I now have tangible evidence that the fence is possessed.

When we took it down it collapsed like a tower of playing cards, every six foot high panel was easier than the last. A four year old could have shoved it over flat, which was partly why we removed it. Trevor has two growing boys who were beginning to size it up.

Even as we carried it away the fence panels were crumbling over our heads, but it was just lulling me into a false sense of security.

For about three months it lay brooding in the pend plotting its counter attack. Its timing couldn't have been better.

One miserable November evening I decided it was time finally to light the stove and so handling my shiny new axe under a maniacal grin I stalked into the pend and eyed my victim. There was a lot more of it than I remembered, at least a dozen or so panels standing upright in three piles.

I tried to pull one out but it played hard to get. No matter which way I wrestled with it the panel refused to budge. I'll be sensible I thought and lay the axe down before I do myself a serious injury. Just to be on the safe side I went off to the shed for a pair thick gardening gloves.

When I returned every single panel had fallen over and the pend was now blocked with a diagonal thicket of larch lap and posts. A few seconds earlier and I would have been buried under the lot.

Somewhere underneath it all lay my axe, so I couldn't even cut my way through it. Just as well because I had underestimated the deadly cunning of my foe.

It took me about half an hour to heave the panels back against the wall, during which a rusty nail went through my left hand glove and slid painlessly between my thumb and index finger. I breathed a sigh of relief; it was a close shave.

So I conceded the first round to the fence and went off to the bunker instead where I knew the coal would at least behave itself.

But I couldn't help thinking the fence had thrown down the gauntlet. It obviously didn't mind being put into retirement but it wasn't keen on being burned.

"You watch what you're doing with fence." Warned my wife as I went into battle a few days later.

This time I decided not to bother moving any of the panels. Instead I sank my axe into the first one that took my fancy. Just as I had hoped the axe head went straight through the brittle larch lap. Unfortunately it went straight though all of the larch lap until it was brought to an abrupt and painful halt by the wall.

As I listened to the sound of crumbling harling the reverberation from the blow shot up my arm like an electric shock and stunned my wrist into feeble submission.

"What have you down now?" Asked my wife as I presented her with my limp wrist.

After that I never found that axe again. It cost me fifteen quid and I only used it once. Just as well my wife hadn't given in to my demands for the big expensive petrol driven chainsaw.

She just laughed when I pointed it out to her in the DIY store and reminded me that it was only an old bit of fence that fell over the moment I looked at it.

The fence didn't look so old and feeble to me now. As the weeks passed it assumed a worryingly defiant air, which I managed to ignore until the snow arrived.

This time I didn't even get a hold of one of the panels, one of the heavy fence posts which I had completely forgotten about jumped me as I was shifting a bag of peat. It slid out of nowhere and as I stepped back, more out of reflex than anything, it caught the front of my left ankle a glancing but teeth clenching blow.

Nervously expecting the worst I inspected it in the privacy of the bathroom, the last thing I wanted was another lecture on fence husbandry from my wife. To my relief all I could see was a slight graze and a little redness. I scoffed at the fence, no contest I said to myself as I slipped my sock back on.

Back out in the pend I ripped a panel apart like a psychopath and grinned with a terrible glee as it blazed in the stove.
Two weeks later I was in Casualty with a septic ankle. Apparently the band-aid I had stuck over the graze hadn't done the trick. The huge Tetanus injection I had to get was the least of my worries.

A doctor had been summoned to tell me there was a chance the poison I had nurtured might get into my bone. There was nowhere else for it to go so the wound would have to be monitored very closely. Then he scrutinised my notes.

"You say a fence post attacked you?" he asked frowning darkly. What could I say? As far as I was concerned I had been ambushed by a big nasty piece of wood.

It was more than a month before my ankle got the all clear. During which time the fence took regular severe beatings from my walking stick and not once did it show any signs of remorse.

Spring arrived and then summer and the stove lay dark and hungry. Then all over Christmas I fought tirelessly with the fence until I had burned it down to the last few remaining panels. I had a catalogue of bruises and scratches, but it was worth it just to see that larch lap catch light in the stove.

Then two weeks ago, just when I thought the fence war was over it bushwhacked me in my own front room. As I snapped a long piece of panelling over my knee it split lengthways and stuck right into the inside of my left wrist.

The Casualty nurse strongly advised me to get rid of the fence. I had to laugh though when she suggested burning it.

Adam's Ale

We've been straining our tap water in one of those jug filters. It's not much bigger than a kettle but it takes ages for the water to filter through it, so if you find it empty you have to shuffle off moaning and find something to do until it fills up, like for instance, watch a double episode of Emmerdale.

The trouble is, when you see the jug is half empty it's tempting to fill it up, but once you've done that, you can't pour out the filtered water that's already there. I've found myself turning it upside down to squeeze out the last drop rather than shove it under the tap.

In a nostalgic sort of way I quite liked the idea at first because it reminded me of camping holidays with my parents. One of the daily rituals involved trekking across a muddy field with my father to a dubious water tap so we could fill an even more dubious looking plastic bottle.

For some reason it was my job to lug the full water bottle back. It was so big and heavy that sometimes I had to drag it. Meanwhile my father would reflect on the general softening up of a society deprived of its primal rights.

About four yards from our tent my father would suddenly relieve me of my burden and get a kiss from my mother for being the big water-fetching hero.

One of those huge water bottles would be perfect but my wife doesn't see the point because she reckons it would take twice as long to fill up. But surely I reasoned, it would take twice as long to empty.

"Exactly," she countered, "And then you would be right back where you started."

This isn't so much filtering as self-imposed rationing, and all for a bargain price of £9.99.

My wife bought the jug in a supermarket because our tap water wasn't exactly what you would call transparent. When you filled a glass it looked like someone had dropped an aspirin in it. Even when it was relatively clear it still had strange little bubbles fizzing around in it that eventually rose en masse to the top and formed a mildly frothy head.

Eventually, if you left the water long enough the bubbles would disappear, but if you shook the glass they came back again, thus offering endless hours of family amusement and discussion.

The filter jug looked pretty insignificant to me and on close inspection appeared to have the inner workings of a jam jar. Even at under a tenner it looked like a con.

After the blind water tasting however it was voted the household's choice. In fact the very first glass from the jug confirmed my wife's suspicions that our water supply was somehow linked to a distant swimming pool.

After more than six years we had obviously grown immune to the taste of chlorine. So much so that our oldest son refuses to drink water from the jug when he's at home because he says it's tasteless.

"Far too bland." He pronounced after swilling the filtered water for the first time over his finely honed palate. "Definitely lacks bite, and the after taste is almost non-existent." He added sourly, as he refilled his glass straight from the tap, much to our horror.

I could barely watch as he cavalierly swigged it back. He then started reflecting on the general softening up of a society deprived of its primal rights and I wondered where I had heard that before.

His protests fell on deaf ears because we had become instant converts to the sacred jug. As far we were concerned we were now the recipients of untainted water. And how right we were because the jug had a nasty surprise in store for us.

Within just a few weeks dozens of gruesome little black specks began appearing at the bottom of the jug. We inspected them like seasoned water detectives, shaking our heads over them in smug 'told you so' silence.

At first I took a typically flippant view, suggesting that we read the black specks like tea leaves to decipher our future, or join them together to see if they form a picture.

But as the days passed and the collection of goodness knows what grew bigger I changed my tune to what can only be described as paranoia in hindsight because we had been drinking our tap water for years without filtering it. Our intake of the little black specks must have amounted to at least a Hoover bag of muck each.

Far from enjoying our daily intake of Adam's purest ale I was now scaring everyone witless. But I just wanted to know what we had done with all those tiny bits of grit and where they had gone.

Before I phoned for an ambulance my wife thought it might be a good idea if we found out where the black specks were coming from in the first place.

So I phoned the North of Scotland Water Authority which incidentally covers an area slightly larger than Denmark and made a casual enquiry about water testing. A lovely chirpy lady on the other end asked where my water came from, and since I wasn't thinking straight I said the tap.

Fortunately she assumed I was a comedian and laughed. She changed her tune though when I told her about the mysterious dark stuff lurking at the bottom of the filter jug and said she would send me some sample bottles for me to fill, which she would then arrange to have collected.

I told her there was no need for that and insisted on sending the bottles back myself, until she reminded me they would be full. She hadn't specified what size of bottles she was going to send but I had in mind something like those giant plastic barrels I used to heave across campsites.

I felt better already. The Authority supplies enough water every day to fill 2,830,000 baths and carries out around 400,000 tests on water quality every year, but they still had time to look into my black bits. However, I didn't realise they were like a negative version of the Fire Brigade.

Twenty minutes later there was a very business-like man on the phone from the Authority.

"I believe you have a problem with your water sir," he said, in a manner serious enough to convince me that I had a very big problem with my water.
"Can I come out today?" he asked and then started talking about doing comprehensive tests – 'not just for lead you understand.'

What could be worse than lead I wondered? And so did my wife. As the Water Authority bloke left with his samples he said that the tests would take about three weeks and if he found bacteria he would come back with bottled water. I was slightly perturbed to hear this but grateful nonetheless.

"Oh no this is terrible," said my wife, "now we'll find out all the stuff we've drinking."

Whoever coined the phrase ignorance is bliss obviously didn't own a water filter jug.

A Bug's Life

It started on a Monday morning with a single, very loud, public sneeze, which according to the old Mother Goose nursery rhyme was a portent of danger. Just my luck, a day later and I would have been kissing a beautiful stranger, and as it turned out infecting them with the nasty virus that was hell-bent on deserting me like a rat from a sinking ship.

Unfortunately my ship had only just sprung a tiny but insidious leak, so it would be some time before I was manning the lifeboats.

First, I had to kid myself on that I was unsinkable. So I went about my business going steadily off channel, like a radio de-tuning itself until I had at least three stations on the go, one of which was definitely the shipping forecast.

Moaning and groaning is never a good way to make pals and it wasn't long before everyone in my office was giving me a wide and wary berth. By lunchtime I was stalking the place like a ghoul ringing a metaphorical plague bell.

I had also developed what my father would have called a starboard list, which worked wonders on the Quasimodo look I had been perfecting.

24 hours after that first sneeze I was firmly back up in the belfry and kissing no one, not unless it was pitch dark because I now looked as if I had been raked over in the middle of the night.

I could vaguely remember the bones of a sweaty nightmare about photocopying myself over and over again until I was left with just a faint washed out sketch. When I woke up I informed my wife that I had run out of toner.

"You can't go into work like that." She said, staring at me as I shuffled round the bedroom like a hedgehog. True I was aching all the way to my fingertips, the result I assumed of my battle with the photocopier and I wasn't making much sense. However, I was in the throes of convincing myself it would pass, probably onto someone else.

For a start I wasn't sneezing and my nose wasn't blocked. My head felt like a bowl of custard, but then you learn to live with these things.

"It's just a bug, I'll be fine," I insisted, slipping on one black shoe and one tan moccasin.

"No, really," continued my wife jumping out of bed to bar the door, "you can't go to work like that, because you've got your melting cheese face on!"

So far I had managed to avoid the mirror. I'd had a sneaking suspicion that it was going to be a melting cheese face day and I felt bad enough without scaring myself.

This is the face I'm normally wearing when I get my photograph taken at parties. Weeks later I'll be shown these photographs and ask who the weird melty guy is getting amorous with my wife. When I discover it's actually me I'm always grateful that people took the time to speak to me.

"You get back to bed," ordered my wife, "and I'll phone the office and tell them you're taking the day off to get a mask fitted."

I realise now that she didn't actually say that last part, but it sounded like it at the time. But then I was so disorientated if someone had told me I was Martine McCutcheon and that I was the star of the new hit production of My Fair Lady everything would have been luvverly.

One of the great joys of being ill is getting someone else to break the news to your work. Normally you're never too ill to pick up a phone and speak for a few seconds, but the mere use of an intermediary adds invaluable weight to the severity of your condition.

On this occasion however, my office would have been more than surprised to hear that Martine McCutcheon was on the phone calling in sick, so my wife did the honours.

I fell back into bed with some reluctance, mainly because it seemed so unjust having a day off and feeling so wretched.

As a distraction I decided to get my laptop out and check my e-mail, but the moment I started replying to the first one I began wroiting in an Oirish accent.

I was baffled. What kind of bug I wondered would make you bi-lingual?

Normally when I'm ill and confined to my bed, which is very rare I have to say, I automatically turn to Sherlock Holmes for comfort. However, in my weakness I picked up the first book that came to a hand.

I could have had a laugh with PG Wodehouse but fate stepped in and dealt me Dorothy Crawford's The Enemy Within, A Natural History of Viruses. I reviewed this lethal little book a few months ago and it frightened into the bathroom where I scrubbed my hands vigorously under scalding water.

My first instinct was to drop the book on the floor. But then I thought, better the enemy you know, and I almost rolled out of bed trying to retrieve it. My wife came in and thought I was trying to escape until I showed her the book. She recommended lots of fluids and paracetamol, but after a brief, heated tug-o-war I won and kept the book.

If nothing else, I reckoned, it might tell me why I had a face like melting cheese. But in reality it was like throwing a drowning man a copy of The Cruel Sea.

Apparently some fifteenth century Italians coined the word influenza believing that flu was caused by a malevolent supernatural influence and seven hundred years later thanks to modern science we know that viruses are too small to argue with.

If a virus were the size of a man then the average bacterium would be the height of the Statue of Liberty. Admittedly this might make treatment a little awkward but it at least puts viruses into perspective.

The most annoying thing about viruses is that they are completely pointless. They can't do anything on their own because they have no brains. Even if every virus in the world teamed up they still couldn't design a Statue of Liberty between the whole lot of them, yet they can make me send someone an e-mail signed, Rudee – it was close enough.

More importantly I discovered that while some viruses make you bedridden so they can multiply in comfort, others con you into believing you're well enough to get up and socialise so you can spread them around.

Whatever it was I was busily increasing it wasn't going much further than my bedroom. Now I felt much better because I didn't feel guilty about not going into my office. How a virus makes you conscientious I have no idea.

I dropped off to sleep holding the book and dreamt I was enjoying a wonderful, aimless and brainless existence, during which I could get away with anything liked, even murder. Martin McCutcheon was still there, singing, "All I want is a room somewhere..."

But that's a bug's life for you.

Saved by the Bell

I could be absolutely anywhere at five o'clock in the morning. Slippery cliff edges used to be a favourite haunt but Submarines are a popular venue at the moment. Particularly if they're filling up with freezing salty water while sinking towards the seabed and I'm trapped behind a huge rusty iron door that I just know will never open. This is an outrageous state of affairs I always think, considering I'm the captain.

Falling down a lift shaft inside a collapsing building is another reliable regular, or being chased naked though a cornfield by apes on horseback. However, it's not all exciting stuff.

Quite often I'm just plain puzzled, knitting my entire being into a knot over a huge life shaping question that I've somehow misplaced, or that I can't see because I'm wearing it as a fruit bowl on my head.

Whatever I'm up to a five in the morning I'm just about ready to be rescued. But over the past few weeks I've been able to retire and dream with complete confidence because I know that when the going gets too weird I'll be saved by the bell.

So far the success rate has been one hundred percent, since as you can probably imagine, nothing tears you from the arms of Morpheus quite like a telephone exploding suddenly into life six inches from your face.

I can remember exactly what I was up to the first time the phone rang in the dead of night, because I thought it was a rather untimely intervention. It was about 4.30 on a Sunday morning and I was at Hugh Hefner's Playboy mansion - researching an article about hot tubs, when one of the bunny girls appeared with a telephone on a silver tray.

I had to get out of the hot tub to get the phone and I just knew I would never get back in again because Mr Hefner's mansion with all its attendant attractions would dissolve around me in a tantalising mist.

By the time I had come to my senses and realised it was my own bedside phone that was going off like a klaxon, my heart was in my throat and I was ready to answer the Phillips emergency action hotline.

Even though the phone was just inches away and sounded as big as a fire engine I snatched up a book, opened it and shouted a panicky hello at about page 82.

Simultaneously, my wife switched on her bedside light and gazed in sleepy amazement as I tried to hold a conversation with a paperback book while an unbelievably loud telephone woke up the entire neighbourhood.

Still holding the book, more out of habit than anything, I grabbed the phone and braced myself, expecting to hear the solemn bearer of bad tidings. Instead there was a full-blown rave-up on the line.

For one bleary moment I thought it was the Playboy mansion trying to woo me back, but no one would speak to me so I never found out. I put the phone down, waited a few seconds and picked it up again just in time to hear a young woman tell someone called Biffo she had lost her drink.

"Do we know anyone called Biffo?" I asked my wife who was clutching her chest in melodramatic anguish.

She shook her head as I listened to the big funky beat down the phone get even bigger and funkier.

"What does he want?" asked my wife, getting more anxious by the moment.

But all I could hear was a lot of wild whooping, like the blood chilling noise made by Red Indians in old westerns when they attacked a wagon circle.

I said I didn't know because he was too busy having a party. My wife thought about this for a moment by staring at the wardrobe door and then flopped back onto her pillow and immediately fell asleep.

I was left listening intently to the rave-up, determined to pick out at least one voice that I recognised but the settlers were now under full attack.

Obviously someone had pressed our number on their mobile by accident. But how eleven digits could be pressed at random and come up with our number was beyond me. Not unless our number had been programmed into the mobile phone's memory.

Perhaps the phone's owner was partaking of a popular groovy dance that presses all the right buttons. My wife's always telling me that certain pieces of music press all her buttons.

Eventually I gave up on Biffo and his war party and went back to bed, but in the morning, or rather three hours later; I dialled 1471 to see if it had recorded the call. To my amazement it had, so I called the number back and needless to say I got an anonymous answering service.

I was going to leave a message asking why we had been called in the middle of the night so we could listen to a horde of revellers having the time of their lives, but I thought that would only invite a flood of phantom party callers.

I needn't have worried. The following weekend at around five am, one of Biffo's pals was playing Fat Boy Slim down the phone at me while a crowd of wild girls laughed themselves off the planet.

Admittedly they had rescued me from a particularly harrowing potholing nightmare, but it was almost as if they were taunting me because I hadn't been invited to their brilliant party. Not that I would have gone anyway, because I didn't know where it was.

This time as I listened closely to the din I became convinced that the party goers weren't having such a great time after all. In fact it sounded a lot like my idea of perfect hell. Not that I'm overly familiar with the noise of people writhing in eternal agony to Hard House music. My wife however, had a better idea.

"Maybe it's the Samaritans doing cold calls, trying to cheer us up." She suggested as I called the number back in the morning. But it wasn't. It was also a different number from the first one. So now it seemed we were dealing with a cartel of accidental nocturnal callers.

I had taken a note of the numbers but everyone in our family shook their heads over them. The mystery deepened last weekend when a girl phoned just after three in the morning from what sounded like a train, albeit a train that was pulling into party central and asked to speak to Biffo.

When I told her she had a wrong number she didn't believe me and insisted that I put Biffo on. Finally she gave up, but warned me that Biffo had to call her back or there would be trouble. I said I would pass on the message.

My son disturbed an entire theatre audience recently with his mobile phone and alarm clock. If this is their idea of revenge, then by my calculations we should have worked our way out of the Dress Circle by Christmas. Or moved house.

Phone Bug

You would almost think we had set a theme for the past month after holding a family ballot to vote for our favourite topics. My car and the central heating system would have been strong contenders. Both had sustained a persistent and convincing presence that inspired harsh words and a regular display of gritted teeth.

But these were both what soap opera writers call back stories. For sheer imagination and cunning brilliance the humble telephone, that most modern of torture instruments proved an outright winner.

First it was an entire theatre disturbed by my son's mobile phone, and I should add his alarm clock which he was carrying around with him in lieu of a watch, but that was just a red herring. Then there's the spate of mysterious nocturnal callers, phoning at 5 am during the weekend so we can listen to them having a rave-up on the other end of the line.

If this is meant to be a from of aversion therapy then it's absolutely hopeless, because my wife and I have started moaning about not being invited to parties. It's almost as if the callers are laughing at us down the line and saying, "Here's another great party you weren't invited to, you sad old gits".

Last Friday night, in anticipation of our regular anonymous caller I tried to convince my wife to let me disconnect the phone, but she said she had been looking forward all week to her 20 seconds of wild night life, so we left the phone alone and no one called.

Obviously the telephone gremlin was resting, recharging his batteries for a full-on assault of impressive proportions. He was going for the big one, but first there would be a nasty little skirmish. The following day he advanced with admirable stealth and struck a potentially lethal blow that stands as a warning to us all.

My wife met a friend for lunch and when their conversation turned to that of another friend, whom they hadn't seen or heard from for several weeks they decided there concern justified calling her right there and then from the café. My wife's mobile was needing re-charged so her friend used hers.

Unfortunately all they got was an answering service. So they left a message and that was that. Or so they thought.

When my wife came home there was a message on our answering machine from the friend she had been trying to contact.
Just to add to the general confusion there were two almost identical messages, one for my wife and one for the friend who had called, suggesting that our number had been dialled a second time by accident.

It didn't matter which message my wife listened to, the effect was the same – an unsettling mix of panic and ceiling scraping hysteria, laced with a sprinkling of even more panic. All of which was unfounded and completely unnecessary, but a lot more exciting than just putting the phone down with a philosophical chuckle.

Apparently when they phoned their friend from the café to find out how she was, they left more than a brief message, they left an entire conversation because they were still on the line. The friend had then arrived home and listened to everything they had said.

Obviously my wife was frantically trying to remember what exactly that conversation consisted of, and for a moment we embarked on a re-enactment of the entire meeting in the café, with me standing in for my wife's friend. But we abandoned it because the phone rang and my wife almost jumped into my arms.

There was a fair chance it was the friend who left the messages and who had listened to the conversation about her so I decided to run away, closely followed by my wife. As it turned out it was a wrong number.

My wife now tried calling the friend she had met in the café to tell her what had happened, but she was out.

There then followed a lot of pacing around interspersed with some fairly tense courtroom drama scenarios until my wife decided that nothing derogatory or untoward had been said about her friend. She had absolutely nothing to worry about, she wasn't a gossip monger and neither was the friend she had met for lunch, they had merely been sharing snippets of news.

"The trouble is, people can so easily misconstrue things." I mused, adding fuel to the now dying fire.

My wife was back on the phone in an instant calling another friend for advice and consolation and I went off to do what I usually do in situations like this, start writing it all down.

Within minutes my wife was poking me on the shoulder and barking in my left ear.

"What have you done to the phone?" she demanded, showing me the phone, but it didn't look any different to me. I just looked at her blankly as she told me how she had been cut off.

I was at a loss to understand how I could have pulled off such a stunt in a room without a telephone but I was happy to take the blame if it meant being left in peace. And it worked, for about five minutes.

That was how long it took our American neighbour, Tool-Time Trevor to knock on our door.

I heard my wife say, "Oh hello Trevor..." and my first thought was, that Trevor's phone must be cut off as well, and that there was obviously a line down somewhere. But then I remembered who I was dealing with and I had a second thought, which was far closer to the truth.

Meanwhile my wife was hitting Trevor with the phone which she was still carrying around in the hope that it would spring back into life. Instead it was now springing off Trevor because in the process of cutting down a tree in his garden he had also cut down our phone line.

Outside in our garden, while I attempted to keep a straight face, poor Trevor tried unsuccessfully to explain to me how he had been harnessed half way up a tree which he had been cutting down. No matter how hard I tried, I just couldn't picture it. One thing was certain; Trevor was lucky to escape with only a broken a telephone line.

I was on the brink of introducing him to the Scottish expression 'big galoot' when he tried to force his mobile into my hand and insisted that I started calling people, anyone he said, phone anyone you like. But I resisted temptation saying that I had to be in the mood, it just wasn't in my nature to make spontaneous phone calls, it was something I had to think about and plan.

So until the phone company turns up with a 100 meters of wire we're marooned in the 19th century writing letters to everyone while a strange sort of peace reigns in the house. In his enthusiasm the telephone gremlin had inadvertently committed suicide. Sometimes you don't know what's been annoying you until it's gone.

Woman with Portfolio

One of my wife's most cherished memories of her recent college course was of being verbally abused down a ventilation pipe. Admittedly at the time my wife and her fellow foundation art students thought they were being playfully cajoled by an invisible omnipresent force.

The class was on a location drawing expedition and had got as far as one of the college entrances when it must have struck them that the ideal location was under their very nose – "The college is positively ringed by illustrative potential," announced one of the young enthusiastic aesthetes. In otherwords it was a bit parky.

So they immediately set up camp and began sketching with earnest fury, as if the blocks of flats and shops in front of them might fly away at any moment like nervous rare birds.

Drawing al fresco in the middle of winter is the perfect way for a busy college to free up a classroom, but not ideal for perfecting your charcoal technique, so in an effort to keep warm some of the artists decided to 'get a fag on' and soon there were little clusters of art appreciation groups discussing the merits of a particular work, while sipping flask hot coffee.

It was then, while the sketchers were immersed in the art of mutual ego massaging that they heard what sounded like a heavenly chorus serenading them from above.

"They were saying something about dodgers." My wife later recalled.

"Jammy dodgers?" I suggested.

"Not quite," frowned my wife, deep in reflective thought.

It turned out the voices belonged to a group of rascally apprentice joiners, who on spotting the happy band of coffee swigging, fag smoking artists outside their building discovered that they could communicate their feelings towards them rather successfully by shouting down a ventilation pipe.

When the artists caught sight of their verbal assailants gesturing through a window, they laughed, but later the doubts set in. Maybe they really were all 'effing dodgers', body swerving the real world of hands on hard graft.

My wife on the other hand took it as confirmation that for the second time in her life she was once again a lazy good for nothing dodger, in otherwords an art student.

However, unlike the young apprentice joiners who were in the process of learning a craft, she was still an apprentice art student.

Although she had been a dodger at Harrogate School of Art in her youth she still had to prove to her new art school that she was worthy of slouching under their hallowed portals and the only way to achieve that was - the portfolio.

The portfolio is the magic carpet that all aspiring art students hope will take them on a journey to art school, that aesthetic Valhalla they dream about every waking and sleeping hour of the day.

The worst part is that the no one can make that magic carpet for you but yourself, and even then it might be earthbound.

This was certainly high on my wife's list of frets and fears because when she had finished compiling her portfolio, although it was held together by magic carpet tape, it was so heavy neither of us could lift it.

It took my wife seven months of dodging about to fill this thing and we couldn't get it into the car. More to the point there was a strong possibility we were going to be sued for inflicting an industrial injury on the art school admissions committee.

Now of course my wife became convinced that she wouldn't get into art school because her portfolio was too heavy.

It took us over two weeks to trim, mount and cover the thirty huge sheets of mounting card that went into the portfolio and the most amazing thing was we were still speaking to one another when it was finished.

After a while I became oblivious to the fact that our entire house looked like an art gallery after an earthquake, because it was such a movable feast.

Every hour or so all the still-lifes, self-portraits – paper party hat obligatory, location and analytical drawings would change places, leaping from the sofa and the table to the floor and even changing rooms.

On the way there was always one or two that would get lost then turn up under an armchair like prodigal sons. Above all others they were cherished and given pride of place, until the next painting disappeared and then turned up after an hour of hand wringing panic and it replaced all the rest as the absolute best thing my wife had ever done.

This is what my wife called her personal selection process, but for me it was a painful re-enactment of the judgement of Solomon.

Criticising your wife's artwork is not something everyone gets to do, or maybe you just don't hear about it very often because no one ever lives long enough to tell the tale.

My method of survival went something like this. Everything was wonderful, but some things were more wonderful than others. The amount of wonderfulness was simply a matter of taste and at the end of the day my wife knew best.

As we tried unsuccessfully to move the portfolio for the umpteenth time I had a brainwave. After checking the application form and finding that there actually was a maximum portfolio weight I dragged out the bathroom scales with a little prayer. Incredibly the portfolio was a gram over the regulation 10 kilos – probably the weight of the portfolio itself I reasoned.

And that is how we decided that my wife's portfolio was ready to go off to art school. It was like weighing a child to see if it was heavy enough for its first day at nursery.

After all the months of work and worry I handed the portfolio over to the art school janitor with no welcoming committee or ceremony, not even a short speech, just a little receipt which my wife later snatched from me to check if it said she had got in.

When she realised it was just a receipt she wanted to know everything that happened - how many other portfolios were there, what did they look like, did I get a chance to open any of them and get a sneaky look at some of the works, what was the janitor like, did he check the portfolio?

I said the janitor weighed the portfolio on a set of bathroom scales he kept under his desk and when he discovered it was a gram over, he rifled through it and pulled out anything he didn't like the look of.

He finally settled on a dramatic ink drawing of a famous cathedral, at which he laughed outloud, then held up for the amusement of passers-by. He finally gave it and a still life featuring a large blue kettle and a rusty old saw the chuck.

The ensuing three weeks seemed like three months and when my wife finally received an unconditional offer of a place at the art school she decided she was a jammy dodger after all. Not yet, I warned, four years of training first.

Facercises

You would think that after 25 years my wife would know whether or not I brushed myself down before having a shower. But then as she often tells me, you need an element of mystery in a marriage.

What you don't need is a big brush scudding across your birthday suit of a morning, not unless you've specifically requested it.

"But it's so good for you," insisted my wife enthusiastically, "So energising and reviving."

The but, tells you how concerned I must have looked. Although I don't know what was alarming me the most, the fact that my wife wasn't sure if I was a pre-shower brushing kind of guy, or that she had obviously tried it herself and found it a rewarding experience.

After giving it a few seconds thought I wondered if it was something you could do in pairs, like mid-sauna birching. But apparently I was never going to find out.

I forgot all about it until I discovered a rather luxurious brush in the shower, the sort of thing a gentleman would use to put a mirror finish on his shoes. Aha, I thought, this explains why my wife always has such an enviable youthful glow.

It also explained why after giving myself a vigorous brushing I was beaming like a human torch. However, I was so pleased with the result I forgot to have a shower, but I do remember thinking it seemed unlikely that my father would ever have buffed himself with a big shoe brush. I also wondered if I should have worked down from my shoulders and missed out my face.

We were in the car when my wife was struck suddenly by the high sheen of my profile and for a moment considered using me as a mirror to retouch her make-up.

"Flipping heck!" she exclaimed, "We are a shiny new person today."

I took this as a compliment and smugly confessed that I had made friends with the shower brush.

When I glanced at my wife for the approval I thought was justly mine she was staring straight at me like Grampa Broon with his falsers out. I was just waiting for her to shout, "C'mer ye wee scoundrel so I can scelp yer lug!"

"What have I done now?" I asked, pre-empting my expectant scelp, but she just kept staring at me like a lipless goldfish, pointing at her face. I was mesmerised, but thankfully she returned to normal in time to warn me that I was hurtling towards a red light.

"I hope your not going to make a habit of that." I said, twitching in my seat.

"Just three times a day." She replied, then pursed her lips tightly together like a disapproving old spinster.

A car pulled up in the inside lane and the driver was just getting interested when my wife relaxed and declared that she felt much better.

I was greatly relieved to hear this, but even more relieved when she told me that I didn't have to brush my face anymore to achieve that youthful healthy glow.

"Facercises," she announced, "That's what you need to do."

I gave her my version of the disapproving old spinster and she congratulated me for making such an admirable first attempt.

"Well done." She said, "Now purse your lips even tighter together and imagine you're crushing a pencil in the middle of them."

I did as I was told, but had to be reminded to keep breathing. Then I had to count to thirty-five until I felt a burning sensation in my upper lip. Which I did, and although it was not entirely pleasant it was certainly preferable to a close-up confrontation with the shower brush.

When I glanced in my rear view mirror I was amazed to find I was wearing someone else's mouth, my lips had literally changed shape and now appeared fuller and more defined.

That was because, my wife explained, I had just performed my first lip shaper exercise, just one of the many natural facelift techniques devised by the American Facercise guru Carole Maggio – 'So easy you can do them in the car'.

Apparently if I continued my Facercise routine for just six weeks I could end up looking like Mick Jagger.

This was too good an offer to turn down, so that evening I sneaked off with my wife's copy of the 'Facercise' book and got down to some serious training in front of the bathroom mirror.

I thought I'd better do a warm up first because I didn't want to wake up in the morning with a permanently pulled face. Carole herself demonstrates some of her easier Facercises on the cover of the book as a teaser, so I copied these.

Pulling a set of faces with her fingers massaging the appropriate muscles, Carole looks as if she's doing a strange version of deaf sign language. If I could have deciphered it I was fairly certain she was saying something like, 'Thankyou for paying £7.99 for this book you wally."

But I decided it was worth it if I was going to be mistaken for Mick Jagger – in his prime of course. Plus, if it worked it was going to be a lot cheaper than a facelift.

I had already mastered the Lip Shaper and was well on the way to developing a nice juicy pout, so next on my list was the Face Slimmer, or the Grampa Broon with his falsers out. All I had to do was open my mouth and forcefully roll my lips over my teeth and then pull the corners of my mouth backwards to my back teeth and roll them in tightly.

This is a lot scarier than it sounds and after frightening myself in the mirror for the allotted thirty-five seconds I decided it would be better if I didn't see what I was doing. But to be honest I didn't mind anyone else seeing me and since Carole has thoughtfully designed many of her Facercises to be done in the car I've now been driving around for the past week looking like a complete lunatic.

You've got to pick your moments though. Particularly if you're practising a Facercise like the Nose Shortener, which involves doing press-ups with the tip of your nose against your forefinger.

After a few days I found I had all the satisfaction of doing a rigorous workout, but with none of the pain. At last I had found the perfect keep-fit regime that would roll back the years, if only from the neck up.

As usual I spoke to soon, or I would have done if I could have moved my jaw because one afternoon I suddenly felt as if my face had gone to the gym for a month and my body had stayed at home with its feet up. When my wife saw me she jumped and shouted, "Blimey for a moment I thought it was Mick Jagger!"

The trouble is, I'm now hooked on Facercises, probably because the adrenaline rush is literally going straight to me head. Nothing to do with vanity of course.

The Microwave

Given enough stupidity you can get used to almost anything, even Sellotaping a microwave shut just to get it to work. The Sellotape was my idea, but in my defence I should say it was merely a design refinement on my wife's original brainwave.

When we discovered the microwave only worked when you forced the door closed I was perfectly happy to wait for three minutes until my thumbs turned white just so I could heat a bowl of soup. By the time the soup was ready my fingers were normally so numb I could hardly hold a spoon, never mind pick up a scalding bowl.

My wife however, took a longer term view. She assures me it's quite awkward cooking with one hand forcing a microwave door shut, so eventually after some highly creative thinking she secured the door with a length of sticking plaster. It was the first thing she found in the drawer under the microwave.

At the time I thought this was ingenious. Apart from the obvious advantage of having a hands-free microwave, there was something particularly satisfying about fixing a broken electrical appliance with a band-aid. It was the sort of thing my father used to do with the radiogram and the television whenever a valve blew, and he was an engineer.

Unfortunately the sticking plasters didn't quite have the lasting power we were hoping for and after a few days we ran out, just as the local shop shut.

I remembered fixing a broken kitchen drawer with Sellotape and being amazed at how well it did the job. That was three houses ago and the Sellotape is probably still in place, preventing a drawer full of someone else's completely useless rubbish from falling into a pile of saucepans.

Millions of words are written every day about DIY and I would bet money that Sellotape hardly gets a mention.

So I produced a roll, placed a cup of water in the microwave, pulled a long strip of tape over the door and pressed the button. Now every time we used the microwave it would be like Christmas morning. The other great thing was, when the tape lost its stickiness you could just pull out a new length, leaving it attached of course to the roll, which would now sit handily on top of the microwave. I had it all worked out.

"There you go," I said to my wife casually, as if it was something I did every day.

It was her turn to be impressed and everyone was happy again, so we celebrated with a daft dance around the kitchen – probably some sort of ancient ritual fire dance thing that's buried in our DNA.

We persevered with the Sellotape for about a month and were on our second roll when my father-in-law pointed out that we were probably unleashing thousands of microwaves around our kitchen because the seal in the door was patently faulty.

It was one of those things you don't think about, but suddenly seemed perfectly reasonable. The real problem was that shopping for a new microwave just wasn't very appealing. Someone was going to have to turn up on our doorstep with the thing before we would give up the Sellotape.

The following evening, the next best thing happened. On a trip to our newly expanded local supermarket we were suddenly halted in our tracks by a huge pile of half price microwaves. Actually it was the price that stopped us.

"24.99!" exclaimed my wife in disbelief. At that price I said we could buy a spare and who cares what they look like as long they work. The woman next to us said she was going to buy three, one for herself and one each for her daughters. We were so excited I remember feeling dizzy with bargain fever.

We couldn't keep the smile of our faces and when we put one in our trolley it felt heavy enough, which I naturally took as some sort of unwritten guarantee of value.

It worked once. Five minutes after I had chucked the old microwave out inside the box of the new one, Mr £24.99 decided it didn't like working in our kitchen. The magic Sellotape was useless because after thirty seconds the bargain microwave of the century ground to a halt whether the door was shut or not. Even our daft dance didn't help and blaming my father-in-law was definitely a mistake.

The supermarket manager was very understanding even when I told him I had binned the box and my receipt. "Don't worry about it," he said, "I know the model you mean."

At the time I was too full of my customer rights to think about what he had said.

The following evening my wife and I were hysterical as we pushed our microwave in a trolley across the supermarket carpark. I couldn't make up my mind if we looked like a pair of refugees or reverse shoplifters, but it was certainly a unique experience, made worse by the fact that the girl at customer services didn't want anything to do with us.

Instead we had to shove the trolley through the shop to the electrical goods counter where a very nice woman apologised for being new and told us we had to go back to customer services. But I wasn't budging because I had spoken to the manager.

"Oh, what did he say?" asked the woman with the sort of genuine interest that only lasts the first day of a new job.

I told her he promised to give us a new widescreen TV as compensation, but she wasn't that new. Instead she presented us with a replacement microwave, which I had to trolley back to customer services so I could convince the first girl I had spoken to that I hadn't nicked it.

She strongly recommended keeping the box and the receipt this time, which didn't sound very promising. She was right of course because Mr £24.99's brother stopped working the moment the bin men took away his box and receipt. At least he worked three times, which was an improvement.

The next day we decided to do the trolley business again under heavy rain, at least it broke the monotony. Why my wife decided to hold the umbrella exclusively over the microwave I never fully grasped. Something to do with rust she said.

There was a different girl on customer services but she wasn't interested either in how many microwaves we had bought, she just wanted to see the box.

"But I didn't buy a box." I said through gritted teeth as my wife dissolved behind me into the supermarket. Then I spotted the first microwave I had taken back, on the floor behind the counter. I thought pointing it out to the girl would help, but she just tried to give me it back.

We wrestled over this for a few minutes until she asked, "So how many microwaves do you need?" It was a good point.

In the end I bought the one I should have bought in the first place and a roll of Sellotape, just to be on the safe side.

On Yer Bike

When I told everyone I had bought a bike they all wanted to know what size of engine it had. For some reason they had difficulty picturing me on a bicycle without laughing hysterically. I didn't think it was that difficult because I was walking around as if I was still on the thing - head stooped forward, knees buckled, buttocks lagging behind nervously. All I had to do was flap my arms and the chicken impression was perfect.

I'd only had my bike two days and I already felt as if I'd had the biggest boot up the backside of my entire life. The strange thing was, I had a suspicion I deserved it, I had definitely earned it.

"Remember, you're doing more good than harm." Assured my wife as we swaggered stiffly away from our bikes like two old cowboys.

The first lesson you learn about cycling is a hard one and it starts from the bottom and works down.

Next to give up hope are your thighs. Apparently you're supposed to perform warm up exercises before you go out on your bike and then warm down afterwards, which doesn't mean standing in front of the stove toasting your behind.

I don't remember any of this when I was young. I just leapt on my trusty Raleigh and took off like a rocket. But the first time I came off my new bike last week I couldn't get up the stairs. My legs just crumpled as if they were made of papier-mâché and it hasn't got any better.

It isn't any easier on the bike either; because suddenly the world is full of hills. We had a vague idea we lived in a valley, but the car has no problem negotiating the almost imperceptible gradients. On a bike it's like climbing Anapurna. Even the slightest incline has to be carefully gauged and measured up as a potential health hazard.

Consequently there are times when it seems my wife and I have bought a pair of bikes just so we can take them for a walk. One evening we met two of our neighbours out with their dogs and the only difference was that our bikes were off the lead.

Needless to say we're completely addicted to our new two-wheeled life. You get a different view of the world from a bike - probably because I keep myself as far away from the seat as possible, so it's a lot easier to be nosy.

Not only can you see into people's gardens and houses, you can also smell and hear them. The countryside around our Steading has opened up during our cycling expeditions like a distant foreign land, peopled with unfamiliar, but friendly inhabitants. Elderly people and children in particular seem to spend a lot of time waving at cyclists.

When the sun's on your bare legs it's also very easy to convince yourself you're one of the Von Trapp family and start singing Doh a Deer.

"Why do I suddenly feel like a German Boy Scout?" was one of my wife's more memorable cycling trip observations. She shouted this as we passed through a bustling quaint hamlet, but the old folk and the kids just smiled and waved.

If we could only have sat down when we got home it would have been perfect.

When I asked the assistant in the bike shop why all the seats were so uncomfortable he grimaced sympathetically, and said that it was probably to stop people from falling asleep. I believed him for a moment and nodded in serious agreement.

I could appreciate that bobbing off when you were riding your bike along a busy road might prove a problem. So having to sit on the best next thing to a knife-edge would certainly focus your mind on the business in hand.

But it turned out most manufacturers put cheap and nasty seats on bikes so you'll go back to a shop and buy an expensive new one.

When they were all hanging up in front of you however, it's impossible to tell, without some kind of pictorial guide, which one would best suit the demands of your posterior.

"What about this one?" I asked my wife, holding up the least lethal seat I could find. Unfortunately it was a ladies, but my wife liked the look of it, because it was the nearest thing to a sofa on display. She took it, but wondered if it was available in a more attractive colour.

Meanwhile I managed to find a gents' seat that promised contour hugging, gel filled luxury and tried to imagine myself bobbing up and down on it by bouncing it in my hand.

My wife thought I was weighing it and not knowing any better, did the same.

"I can't see what good this is doing." She said after a few minutes. I didn't either but I couldn't think of an alternative. I had a quick look round the shop and confirmed that all the bikes for sale had evil looking seats so there was no point in testing any of them.

My wife tried fitting her seat under her behind but that didn't help much so I offered to hold it so she could sit on it. But that wasn't much good either so I held her seat on my knee and she sat on it gingerly.

By this time the sales assistant had spotted us and rushed over to reassure us that we could take the seats back if we didn't like them. I think we were alarming the other customers who had children with them.

We bought a set of spanners just to look as if we knew what we were doing.

Unconvinced by this, the sales assistant ran through the process, which I had completely forgotten by the time we got home.

I never got Meccano for my Christmas, I was more a Lego man and I can understand now why this worried my father. But in a strange way I almost enjoyed taking our bikes apart and fitting them together again, it was an interesting way to spend two hours and allowed me to bond with our bikes.

Fuelled by my success and now travelling under the new title of Head Bicycle Repair Man we set off to test our new seats at a local park, where at least the only danger would be posed by ourselves.

Unfortunately they were still unrelenting. Going up the first hill I heard my wife scream and turned round to find her sitting on her rear wheel with her seat pointing up towards her chin. Just as I was about to stop I crested the hill and hurtled down the other side and my handlebars, which I had raised, sank like a lead weight.

Miles form home we had no option but to persevere. My wife rode her bike as if she was sitting on a see-saw while I spent a lot of time staring at the ground.

I had my spanners confiscated, but the open road still beckons. Once I can ride my bike without wearing eight pairs of pants it will be wonderful.

Thirty Thousand Lives

I think some strange mysterious force drew me to the Body and Soul Health Fair. All morning I'd been doing my best to resist it but I was fighting a losing battle. One minute the trip was off the next it was on. Every excuse I came up with sprang a leak. Obviously I just didn't know my own mind.

By two o'clock on a wet Sunday afternoon the Fair was heaving. Mostly with women. The few men I could see were hunting through the stalls of crystals and alternative remedies with a focussed purpose. As usual I was looking for a story, and I certainly found one.

At the time I thought I was lucky not to have missed it. But later I realised there was never any doubt I was going to meet Evinu.

Even though he was sitting, tucked away in a corner, busy drawing, I saw him the moment I walked in and our eyes met in time-honoured fashion across a crowded room.

It probably had a lot to do with the poster beside him that promised, 'Past Life Drawings'. Since he was alone I assumed he was drawing one of his own past lives, but if that had been the case he would have been sketching for at least the next millennia. According to his story he might well be.

When he glanced up our stares locked for too long until I broke away and dived into the Fair, immersing myself in the heady scent of incense and the drowsy drone of bees and birdsong.

I filed him and put him to the back of my mind - as you do when you're shopping in the hope that something better comes along. In truth I wasn't ready for him. First I had to prepare myself by travelling back in time to the present for some thought provoking ritual browsing.

So I learned a thing or two about Druids, watched a 45 year old Grandmother of three who is about to discover a new man in her life having her destiny unveiled publicly by a Tarot card reader and then picked up an Angel Card which advised me to be more understanding. It was already happening.

Just an hour spent at one of these Mind and Body events is a tonic in itself. Watching complete strangers lying flaked out on couches having their daily stresses massaged out of them, or being faith healed by other people who look like they've fallen asleep standing up, can be extremely relaxing.

Obviously there is an element of osmosis at work with these things, because I began to feel pretty chilled out as I strolled around through the gently eccentric crowd. Lulled by the soothing pan pipe music and the seductive bouquets of the aromatherapists I just blended in, which, when you think about it, is probably as good as it gets.

In fact I was so relaxed and so charmed by the strangeness of it all that when I heard someone call my name I thought I was hearing voices and I had to dig my way back up to the surface reality. It was like being lost in a crowd and then found by a familiar smiling face.

As far as I was concerned Alison Clark was a computer wizard–she played a key role in setting up the IT at the new Hong Kong airport, so I assumed she had been dragged to the Fair by a wacky mate.

She was one of the exhibitors. Alison now spends half her week fixing computers and the other half fixing people. It's an excellent arrangement since she works in a highly pressured business environment full of stressed out potential patients desperate for her skills as a Shiatsu expert.

She offered me a free on-the-spot acupressure session, and though tempted I sensed I had a prior engagement.

Back in his corner Evinu – given name Lewis Ballantine, had just completed another past life drawing and an ecstatic customer was leaving with it rolled up under her arm. She obviously couldn't wait to show her chums. I didn't see it, but I imagine it confirmed her suspicion that she had been the Queen of Sheba.

I introduced myself; notebook in hand and Evinu offered me a seat while he leaned against the wall. A small, slightly built bearded man with a ponytail, he looked to me like a folk musician. His eyes were incredibly calm and deep set and he had a Roman nose that made him look at once hawk like and scholarly.

When I asked him to tell me about himself he asked which one. I laughed and told him to pick a number.

"Oh just the same as everyone else" he said, "Twenty to thirty thousand, not all as people of course, I've been many different animals."

Admittedly the number got my attention but it was his demeanour that really impressed me, because he acted as if he was discussing something totally urbane, like shoes or cars. When I asked how he knew about his thirty thousand lives he just laughed lightly, as if I should know better.

He then told me about his spiritual name Evinu and its origin, as if that would clear things up. Apparently he had been a

Cherokee Indian called Yellow Hawk and he had arrived on earth a long time ago from another planet as a ball of energy about 18 inches in diameter.

Back in his present life in 1984, he was driving a bus for the disabled when he read a newspaper ad for a spiritual awareness seminar. A few months later his life, or rather his lives had assumed an astonishing depth.

Now, he was a successful psychic healer, based in Edinburgh. He healed everything including trees.

"Why not?" he asked shrugging his shoulders, as if it was the least he could do.

Distance healing and psychic surgery were his specialities. I got the feeling the past lives drawings were just an amusement. They were also a cleverly baited hook that caught people.

Few of them ever got as far as me though. Evinu was holding up a large black and white photograph of himself in a pith helmet, only it wasn't him, it was Lord Wingate. There were others, he had an extensive portfolio, including a statue of a Gaul chieftain who fought the Romans. In every case I had to admit the resemblance was uncanny.

Just before I left, Evinu turned the tables and told me I had been a bear three or four times, a beaver an elephant and more significantly, a male in ancient Egypt. Now I felt like the woman with her rolled up drawing.

Back home, looking at all the leaflets I had collected – everyone has a leaflet, I caught myself toying with one of the ancient little statues that live on my desk. I had to smile when I realised what it was. A fat crouching gold Ibis with a turquoise beak he was known as Thoth. He was the god of writers and was worshipped widely throughout all Egypt.

The Clockwork Orange

I've been taking Ginkgo Biloba; it's an extract of the world's oldest living tree species and for the past five thousand years Chinese herbalists have been recommending its memory improving properties. But I must have forgotten to take it because I don't think it's working.

I was standing on a platform of the Glasgow Underground last Saturday afternoon when I remembered I hated tunnels.

"Wait a minute," I said outloud, "I hate tunnels."

It must have occurred to my wife around the same time because she was holding my hand. No wonder, to my absolute incredulity I was standing about thirty feet under Glasgow's Kelvinhall. More to the point, I was awake - normally I'm asleep when this happens and in the middle of a nightmare.

You would have thought the word Underground might have been a hint, but we just swept along the street, bought a couple of tickets for something called 'the clockwork orange' and then trooped down an innocuous flight of stairs behind a bunch of kids.

My wife and I were chatting away quite happily for a few minutes before I realised I was buried alive in a dank crypt under the street. But I was willing to give it a chance. Maybe it was time for me to face my primal fear, but it's more likely I didn't want to make a prat of myself in front of a crowd of kids and young women.

So I looked around and weighed up my chances of survival. I had to admit they were probably quite high, but that didn't mean I had to enjoy it.

The funny thing was we had just left a very similar environment and it hadn't bothered me in the slightest, probably because it was above ground.

We had been exploring the Kelvingrove Art Gallery, one of my wife's childhood haunts – every time she visits it now she hears Beatles' songs in her head.

A sprawling red building it sits in its lush park like a grand sanatorium, but inside it's a cross between a Victorian railway station and a Synagogue.
Huge gold lanterns hang from the overly decorated vaulted ceiling around which the names of composers, some misspelt – Palestrino, Scarletti... are carved next to the city guilds – Skinner, Weaver, Tailor. In the empire's cathedrals of learning everyone could be a genius.

On the ground floor a stuffed zoo and sinister suits of armour rub shoulders with iron age artefacts while in the airy café a waitress holds up a plate for public inspection shouting, "Zennay-wun lookin furra curry?" There are no takers.

A boyish Rembrandt in a feathered hat smiles down on this scene from a gilt frame that looks as if it once belonged to a mirror. This upper corridor is packed to the ceiling with a pick n'mix of pile 'em high pictures, sustaining the Victorian ethic of value for money. And everywhere there are stone arches that turn into gloomy tunnels just to keep you focussed on the road to enlightenment.

The gallery opened in 1901 but thoroughly modern Glaswegians had already been riding the underground for five years – at the Buchanan Street station one of the original wooden cars has been sliced in half and bolted to the wall as a reminder that style was once married to function.

More than a century later the Glasgow Underground is still the only passenger carrying tube line outside London. It certainly seemed an attractive alternative to the traffic jammed buses we walked passed.

The doorman at the Art Gallery told us with a sly wink to leave our car in his free car park and take the clockwork orange into the city centre – fast and cheap he said. He was right on all counts.

A few dozen people had gathered on the platform which can't be more than 8 feet wide. With a deep waterlogged track on either side it wasn't hard to imagine someone being nudged into the path of an oncoming train. Murder, or unfortunate accident? It would be hard to tell.

It was also hard to nail the inescapable smell. Not exactly like a drain, more like a mausoleum, or even a church organ loft, it was worrying whatever it reminded you of. It was also suspiciously warm, as if we were near the big underground boiler room that in my imagination heated the city.

I looked into the dark pools of the twin tunnels around which were painted the words, 'there's one coming any minute' and shuddered. Whoever dreamt that one up had a warped sense of humour.

But they were right. We had only been waiting a few minutes when a powerful rush of wind blew re-designed everyone's hair. Then a jet began to fly directly over our heads. Nobody batted an eyelid, they were too busy re-arranging their hair, so I held tight convinced that any moment we would all duck in unison.

While I braced myself for impact a tiny orange train roared out of a tunnel and ground to a screaming halt.

It was definitely orange and it ran like clockwork, the key at the end of it probably wasn't as big as I had first thought. Through the windows I could see real sized people like us, but they had obviously been folded up to squeeze inside.

Some of them slipped out and resumed their normal shape before carrying on their journey. We ducked as we entered the nearest car and kept ducking until we found some empty seats. For some reason I had to sit opposite the dazed drooling young man who had recently been the victim of a practical joke involving collagen lip implants.

Thankfully he liked the look of me. In my state of extreme faked relaxation I think he mistook me for a spaced-out kindred spirit.

The first thing I learned about the underground train is that it takes off as if it's in a cartoon – it takes a deep breath, then lurches back before shooting off like a bullet and firing its passengers in the opposite direction.

The tunnel eats it up with no room to spare and the temptation to make yourself smaller would be irresistible if you weren't still busy making new friends.

I have to say I've been on funpark thrill rides that are less exciting. The car in front wobbled from side to side like a high-speed jelly while ours seemed to just jump around in the direction most likely to make you sick. The constant jet engine noise however put paid to any form of verbal moaning. So I was reduced to making brave smiles while doing my best to avoid dribbly boy's stare.

All of this explains why I didn't see any senior citizens on the train. By the time they reached their destination – in ten minutes flat, their would be very little of them left intact.

When we stumbled out into the heaving throng of Buchanan Street my wife wondered if my aversion therapy had worked, but I was too stunned to speak.

"Never mind," she said, "The return journey might do the trick."

Another thing that had slipped my mind.

On The Buses

My wife assured me that once you learn to ride a bus you never forget, but I still wasn't convinced. I think she was getting confused with bikes.

I had been trying to come with up an excuse for not taking the Park and Ride bus into town to do our Saturday afternoon shopping and my last and best shot – after our car being pinched, and the bus being hijacked by militant extremists had been actual bodily harm.

"When was the last time you saw someone injured on a bus?" asked my wife.

I couldn't come up with an exact date but it was probably the last time I was on a bus - about twenty years ago.

"Buses are dangerous things," I said, "They pull out in front of you at roundabouts."

Reluctantly I drove into the car park and for a moment I perked up because it looked full. Then some joker thoughtlessly reversed out of a space just yards away and I had no option but to pull in.

For years I've driven into town on Saturdays and felt duty bound to moan about the heavy traffic, the incompetence of other drivers, the exhaust fumes, the lack of parking, the heavy traffic, the incompetence of other drivers...

Taking the Park and Ride just didn't feature in my vicious circle.

"Basically," reasoned my wife, "It's all about relinquishing control. You need to be the master of your own destiny, the man behind the wheel, but in order to move on you must give yourself up. Only then will you be able to find yourself again."

I was half listening to this Taoist take on the art of bus travel while pretending to scour the car for ticket machine change, but by a complete stroke of luck the car appeared to have been sucked dry of its usual float.

"And don't bother pretending you don't have any change," added my wife, "Because I've got it already." Then she left to feed the nearest machine.

As I waited I decided my aversion to the Park and Ride had something to do with being mentally and physically scarred for life during a childhood spent waiting in the rain for late buses and then being berated by irascible drivers hell-bent on shaking the life out of their passengers.

I've still got the chipped front tooth to prove it. I scowled at it in my rear view mirror, and wondered where my adult guardian was when I was biting the metal rail of the seat in front?

I also once fell off a bus as it hurtled round a corner. All my pals laughed and the conductor shouted after me as I stumbled to the ground, informing me that I wasn't allowed to jump off the bus between stops.

"We know where he lives!" chorused my so-called mates as I picked myself up wincing at the tarmac now buried in my knees and palms. A kindly old lady came up and gave me my bashed schoolbag, but then she scolded me and hoped that I had learned a valuable lesson.

I certainly had. Since then there has been a strong association in my mind between buses and public humiliation.

I was forced out of this nostalgic reverie when my wife returned with a free Park and Ride ticket given to her by some bloke who had a convoluted tale which neither of us understood. He was obviously a man after my own heart who needed to be the master of his own wheels.

There was no arguing now. The nice gleaming bus had just arrived and as far as we were concerned it was free, like some introductory offer. There had to be a catch I thought, as I warily climbed onboard.

The bus certainly looked suspiciously clean and customer friendly, as did the driver. When he greeted every passenger with a broad handsome smile I went on red alert.

My wife decided she would ask him for the time of the last bus back from town and rather than point gruffly at the timetable outside he was incredibly pleasant and chatty. I watched from my seat as they joked and laughed together. I waited for him to turn on her with that familiar threatening scowl, but they parted the best of pals.

I wasn't sure what his game was. Either it was his first day on the job or he fancied my wife, possibly both. Whatever the reason for his boundless conviviality he wasn't fooling me and I was keeping a close eye on him.

"Things are very different now," reassured my wife, returning to her seat, "It's a shiny new world of customer care."

There were still no seat belts, but the chances of ruining your dentures were slim. Practically the entire bus was made of plastic, if it hit deep water it probably would have floated.

As we sailed past the traffic jams like VIPs my earlier worries about the nice driver turning round suddenly with a skull face and driving us to Hell were beginning to fade.

My wife had also been right about losing control, and finding myself again. When I stood near up our stop I had no control over which direction my body went. I seemed to be particularly interested in crashing into the woman behind me and the bloke in front, both of whom had mastered the art of balancing upright in a moving vehicle.

While I performed an old mannie version of the Michael Jackson moonwalk the rest of the standing passengers – including my serene wife swayed like reeds in the wind. The secret is to go with the flow, bend or break, or in my case, bend or breakdance.

Then I found myself again, right outside the first shop I wanted to visit. I was elated, but I think that was more to do with the fact that I had survived my first bus ride in twenty years.

"And the driver was so nice." said my wife.

The following weekend we went back for a repeat performance. This time we had to buy a ticket. We hung around the machine until the bus arrived but no mysterious benefactors turned up. Still, the driver was pleasant, a cosy old uncle type who pulled faces at the kids and I was looking forward to showing off my moondance – I'd been practising some new moves.

We had a care-free shopping trip in town and the Park and Ride bus turned up on time to take us back to our car. As we boarded the bus my wife showed the driver our ticket and he asked for the other one, apparently everyone is meant to have their own ticket, it doesn't cost you any more and you can have up to five.

But we had broken the rules and in order that we wouldn't forget next time the driver threw a little tantrum. It was just enough to restore my faith in human nature.

We're going to persist with the Park and Ride. Apart from the obvious benefits, you get a better view from a bus.

The Haunted TV

I never think I've video recorded a TV programme properly unless I've set the timer to stop at least three minutes before the end. I have no idea how I do it, but it's obviously a deep inner need for suspense.

I've lost count of the amount of nail-biting thrillers I've never seen the end of. My wife now braces herself for that abrupt cut into the middle of an old episode of Coronation Street that we've seen ten times before. In fact our evening wouldn't be complete without our regular sofa discussion on who did what to whom and who married who in the end.

The next morning we trawl round people to find out how close our deductions actually were. If we can't find anyone who saw the same programme we'll call the TV production company. I've spoken to the same girl at Granada so often we're on first name terms.

My wife and I have grown to live with the fact that our video recorder has a mind of it's own, a sort of built in censor designed to keep us on the edge of our seat. But then it embarked on some kind of expansion plan and roped in our TV with infuriating results.

The first sign that we were dealing with a force greater than ourselves happened during the Six o'clock news. Right in the middle of yet another harrowing report about a riot the television decided enough was enough and switched itself off.

For a moment I was relieved, but my wife just assumed I was up to my old tricks because normally when this sort of thing happens it turns out I'm sitting on the remote control. The poor remote gets a rough time of it in our house, no more so than when it's being suffocated under my behind.

Once its exact whereabouts are located a subtle twitch of the cheek in question and the TV springs back into action. It's simply a matter of the appliance of pressure on science.

This time the TV decided it couldn't wait and came back on by itself and just in case we were going to watch that horrible riot again it changed the channel. One minute the screen was black and the next we were watching an old Western.

"That was clever," declared my wife staring at a herd of stampeding steers. "You've certainly got the measure of that remote."
I certainly had. In fact I had surprised myself. I'd just spotted the remote balancing precariously on the edge of the coffee table and was in the process of reaching for it when the TV came back on. All I had done was move forward a few inches. Now that's what I call remote control.

"Any chance you can flex the other cheek and get the news back on?" asked my wife.

I did my best but failed miserably.

Half an hour later the TV decided it didn't like the look of the weather report. One minute the sun was shining pointlessly over the North Sea while a cold front advanced from the West and the next the screen was black.

My wife stared at me. "Getting fed up now," she announced as the TV came back on and we were watching The Simpsons.

After that initial spectacular show of self will and defiance the TV took a well-earned rest for about a week. Just long enough for us to believe that normal service had been resumed.

Of course it was just biding its time, waiting for the most annoying moment to strike.

We had spent about an hour and a half one evening arguing about the outcome of a gripping thriller and just as the detectives were about to reveal the identity of the murderer and my wife was about to say, "Told you so!" we were looking at that black screen again.

My wife leapt to her feet and we were watching the golf. By the time we had dug the remote control out from under the cushions and dropped it twice before turning the channel, the end credits of the thriller were rolling.

Over the weekend it happened so often we were past caring, we were happy enough for the TV just to come back on.

But then it started coming back on, even when it wasn't meant to be on in the first place.

We were in the kitchen when Top of the Pops suddenly began blaring rap music from the front room. I don't know what we thought we were going to find but we crept back into that room like a pair of SAS men on a moonlit raid.

The next day it was a toss up between calling the TV rental company or a priest.

A very young man turned up to sort out the unruly set. In fact he looked so young that when I showed him into the front room I waited for his dad to follow behind, but Junior was all I was getting.

"This TV has a mind of its own." I warned, trying to give him some idea of what he was up against, but he just narrowed his gaze and nodded his head.

"We'll see about that." He snarled, whipping out his screwdriver.

But half an hour later, with the TV in several nasty looking chunks Junior was on the brink of admitting defeat.

"Mind of its own?" I asked, but Junior shook his head over the gutted set.

"Sunstroke," he announced grimly.

For some reason this sounded worse than being haunted. But apparently it was ingeniously simple. The back of the set faced our patio windows and on sunny days – there have been two in recent living memory, the TV overheats, then cools down again making spontaneous connections in the process. Junior's version was far more interesting.

The bad news was the TV had to be taken away to recover, probably in a temperature controlled, darkened environment. Junior however had brought a replacement set with him.

He wired it up and we discussed the finer points of televisual physics as a cricket match played in the background. I was delighted; the grass was greener on this set than it was on ours.

Just as Junior was packing up, promising to have our set back in working order by the middle of the week the screen on the replacement TV went blank for a moment and then a black and white Cary Grant film flickered to life.

When Junior carried the replacement set out to his van I could have sworn I heard him speaking to it, but maybe he was just talking to himself. Our house tends to have that effect on visitors. I had told him to have both TVs exorcised so maybe that was what set him off.

There is of course a rational electrical explanation for this, but who cares?

The common denominator between both sets of course was the remote control. From now on nobody sits on it, throws it around the room or slaps it when it refuses to work. It will be handled with kid gloves and the fear it deserves.

Asking for Trouble

My wife says that sometimes I go around asking for trouble, not actually physically going up to complete strangers and insisting on a bout of impromptu strife. It's subtler than that, it must be because apparently I don't realise I'm doing it.

Just last week I was at it again and all because this bloke knocked on the door. He was wearing a baseball cap covered with badges and a brown leather waistcoat unbuttoned over a whitish tee-shirt advertising a well known brand of cider.

I was so busy looking at this get-up that I didn't clock the bloke's face. Consequently when my wife asked me later if he looked like a potential burglar I couldn't give her a convincing answer. So I got a row and a Neighbourhood Watch lecture.

"I just happened to be passing," said the bloke fidgeting with something in his waistcoat pocket, "And I noticed the trees around your garden are needing cut."

He motioned behind him in case I was in any doubt about which big trees he meant.

I thanked him for sharing his concern, he nodded and smiled and I closed the door. But there was obviously something else he wanted to get off his chest because I was barely out of the vestibule when he was knocking on the door again.

The upshot was that he wanted to cut the trees for me in exchange for £450. That was about ten quid a tree and probably more than each tree cost when they were planted 20 years ago.

"Well, it's a lot of work," he said justifying his estimate, "And it might be quite tricky."

I said I would be back in touch if I got government funding.

What I couldn't fathom was why he thought the trees needed cut in the first place. They're about 25 feet high but if they weren't they would be shrubs. On one side they stare at the road and on the other into our garden. They don't shield the sun, on the rare occasions when it deigns to come out but they are highly effective as a gale break.

But this encounter planted a seed of doubt, which by mid afternoon had grown to such a size that I had gone rummaging for the hedge clippers. This apparently is how I ask for trouble without saying a single word.

Everyone had gone out by this time so I was also left to my own devices, another personal problem area fraught with hidden pitfalls.

I had no intention of lopping the tops of the trees, I wasn't feeling that energetic, I just fancied giving the few trees that march down our drive a number two, or three, depending on how quickly I remembered I had something more interesting to do.

The trouble is, once you start trimming trees or hedging and the neater it gets, the scruffier the next bit looks. It's also surprisingly addictive.

In about half an hour I had trimmed the trees as high above my head as I could reach without my arms popping out of my sockets and the drive was now a delicious mass of slippery green cuttings.

It also looked as if it had grown a huge green balcony. I inspected it from several angles trying to determine whether my wife would notice it or not, but there was no escaping it, when she arrived home she would drive underneath it and duck.

Even from my point of view this was a disaster, because I had gone too far, but not far enough.

There was nothing else for it, the extendable ladders had to be dragged out and coerced with strong language into extending. I expended more energy doing this than I had done working the clippers, but eventually I had the ladders out to their full length.

The real problem was what to lean them against. To me the answer was obvious, but it contravened every health and safety rule of the household.

The only thing I had to fall back on, apart from the drive was the excuse that nobody was around to give me a hand so I had no option but to prop the ladders up against the trees themselves.

It was an interesting idea and at first seemed reasonably sound. Once the top of the ladder was stable against some branches up I went, rather stealthily I might add because the ladder was bouncing.

About fifteen feet up I lost my nerve and I had to drop the shears in order to grab the nearest branch to stop myself falling off.

The shears got wedged half way down inside a tree and to retrieve them I had to go back down and then fight my way up through a thick mesh of branches and scratch myself for Britain.

Undeterred I climbed back up the ladder. I realise now I was asking for trouble with a vengeance but it still came as a surprise.

Unfortunately I was lured into a false sense of security – literally.

I was happily chopping away, but straining to reach far too high above my head so up I went in hot pursuit of the top branches. It was then the ladders took a sickening lurch forward, but then they steadied themselves again so I carried on as if nothing had happened. The next lurch was more serious and the top of the ladder vanished into the green mansion above me, but still I persisted thinking, 'what's the worst that can happen?'.

When the ladder twisted suddenly I had a vision of the shape of things to come, which involved me being trapped like a helpless fly in a spiky web of branches.

I weighed up the appeal of this and decided to jump for it. I must have climbed a lot higher than I realised because the ground was nowhere near where I left it.

Time and after time I braced myself for the impact but I just kept going, free-falling in slow motion towards the branch-strewn gravel.

When I eventually landed the soles of my feet hurtled up to scream at my knee caps and the shockwave ran right up to the back of my head. But I was all right and still standing. It was then that I admitted that I had been asking for it. And as if by magic down it came.

After I had jumped off the ladders they must have rebounded and then followed me down a few seconds later. As I stood there in a daze, the ladders hurtled past within an inch of my right ear and crashed on the ground. I jumped with fright, slipped on the branch cuttings and ended up on my backside with my arms folded over my head.

A few seconds later and the ladders would have landed on top me as I lay on the roof of my wife's car. She had arrived home right on cue.

She didn't have to say it this time. A look was all I got. And I was right about the green balcony; she wasn't impressed with that either.

The Accidental Americans

When someone is telling you in a foreign language how to work an entire kitchen full of electrical appliances I find it easier just to nod and smile and get rid of them as painlessly as possible so I can get on with the job in hand, for example, being on holiday and enjoying myself.

Who cares if you can't work the toaster, you can always burn some bread on the barbie.

Or alternatively, as my wife usually does, you can spend the first few hours of your holiday coming to grips with the finer points of the kitchen. If I leave her alone long enough this usually does the trick.

But after another day without hot food, hot water, and an ice cube that didn't turn into a puddle in the palm of your hand we began to feel a little unchilled to say the least. Even the shower in our lovely rustic Tuscan villa which had promised a hair parting deluge turned out to be an absolute drip.

We did manage to light the gas hob, but only after draining two lighters – souvenirs of Pisa Airport and a large box of Vatican City Matches – St. Peters on one side, Sistine Chapel Ceiling on the other.

The oven however, remained as mysterious and dark as an Etruscan Tomb. Even my tried and tested method of pressing every button and turning every dial in every sequence I could think of had failed miserably.

"But what did the man say?" insisted my wife through gritted teeth.

I couldn't honestly say, except for the fact that he wondered what part of America we were from.

Which wasn't much help in the confusing world of Italian kitchen appliances.

The bloke in question was Maurizio; the big built black-bearded genial handyman. No one quite knew the true depths of his usefulness, but you just had to look at him and you could tell that one day he would come in handy.

For us, that day arrived when we attempted to abduct an umbrella with a two-ton weight on the end of it from the swimming pool.

We couldn't possibly have carried such a mighty thing to our courtyard so I concocted a devious plan involving reversing the car to within a splash of the pool and then heaving the brolly and the weight into the boot.

But Maurizio rumbled us, "you crazy Americanos!" he laughed and fetched a wheelbarrow.

When he lifted up the two ton weight with one hand and stood toying mindlessly with it while I pondered over the ideal spot for the brolly I thought, that's handy.

Unfortunately Maurizio's Kryptonite was our front door because whenever he stepped over our threshold he was robbed instantly of his super handy powers.

First of all there was a lot of shuffling about and smiling to get through and several sections of the phrase book and to be honest I thought I was getting somewhere but my wife wasn't so convinced.

"For goodness sake just tell him everything's broken before I lose the will to live!" she shouted.

Maurizio just smiled. I had a feeling he had heard this before.

Realising the extent of our plight he then went into top gear which really just amounted to the same old round of head scratching and beard rubbing. There was one exciting moment when we thought he had made a breakthrough but he was just pausing to pull up his shorts.

He did however, remove his black sunspecs – on my recommendation, when he peered inside the oven. But still he could see nothing.

When I held a lit match inside the oven he took it from me and muttered into the black abyss for a long time as if deciphering some ancient obscure language. I knew the feeling.

The diagnosis was not good. Basically because it was Sunday. At first we wondered if kitchens weren't allowed to work on a Sunday because of religious grounds, but when Maurizio said 'Domani' everything became clear and our hopes sank.

He meant of course that we would have to wait until 'Domani' or tomorrow, for a tradesman to come and fix everything. Everyone knows that 'Domani' never comes so I decided to take matters into my own hands.

The tall nice lady from Hull next door was basking in the courtyard outside casually hoovering up the splendid Tuscan twilight. She was obviously having a moment. Hundreds of House Martins were playing above the Loggia before retiring for the night. The valleys to the east had turned purple and the tiny lights of distant hilltop towns were beginning to twinkle like freshly fallen stars.

"Oh, ello luvee, isn't this sublime?" she enthused over a glass of dark Chianti.

"Yes sublime," I agreed brusquely, "Have you managed to light your oven yet?"

She smiled up at me slowly and rather suggestively and said, "getting there." Which I took as a no, at least she had the right attitude.

Back in our kitchen the atmosphere was not quite so tranquil. My wife had finished negotiating with the boiler and had advanced onto terror tactics. This involved counting to ten before thumping the boiler with the big old Espresso maker.

"Don't worry," said my wife, now wide eyed with frustration; "The Espresso maker doesn't work either!" This was little consolation.

Apparently the boiler was meant to spring into life the moment any of the hot taps were turned on, but it just hung there on the wall completely comatose. It was almost as if the kitchen had gone on holiday somewhere else.

Short of anything better to do I decided I would get up on a chair to investigate the boiler, at least from this vantage point I could disarm my wife of the dud Espresso maker.

It was then I noticed what looked like a rather unusual set of dominoes built into the wall tiles above the work surface.

"These are strange." I said.

"Yeah, and they're loose," moaned my wife, "They move about, look..."

They turned out to be the control switches for everything my wife had inadvertently turned off the moment we had arrived.

In her defence they had been fitted upside down, so even if she had realised they were switches, she would have still switched everything off.

Suddenly the kitchen was humming with life, the fridge was purring, the toaster popped non-existence toast and at the first twist of the hot tap the boiler gave a loud burp and fired up. More surprisingly the oven came on, because of course it was electric.

When Maurizio knocked on our door in the morning with news of an approaching electrician he found a scene of hot breakfast bliss. I gave him a slice of toast and told him I had fixed everything myself.

He grinned broadly, shook my hand then wagged a knowing finger at me. "Smart Americano." He said and ambled off crunching his toast.

I had a feeling this was a reputation I was not going to live up to.

Cock-Up

As dreams go there was nothing particularly unusual about this one.

I was driving across a desert in a vintage car and I couldn't stop the horrible horn honking. It was one of those horns that sounded like it should be on a pompous little tugboat that had ideas above its berth. A ghastly cross between a Victorian factory klaxon and a blood-chilling scream.

Why this horn persisted in blasting off I had no idea, but it was driving me mad. The road – if you could call it a road, was empty as far as the eye could see. In fact the desert was appropriately deserted, apart from myself and of course my wife, I had a notion she was somewhere around, possibly asleep in the seat next to me.

Which is why I was so annoyed about this noisy horn. It seemed hell-bent on waking up my wife and the rest of the world with her, whoever they might be.

Apart form the horn going off and the all-enveloping extra wardrobe of stifling heat that was it really.

I had a vague notion that I was in a pool of sweat but that was hardly surprising considering the heat. Someone it seemed to me had accidentally turned the sun full on.

I don't often dream about driving vintage cars across deserts which is probably why I didn't realise it was a dream. The horn also sounded too real for a dream, which of course it was.

While I was struggling to drive in a straight line my wife was dreaming about buying gallons of honey and lemon cough medicine and throat pastilles. Someone in the neighbourhood had the most terrible sore throat she had ever heard and it was hurting her throat just listening to them.

Meanwhile back in the real world it was about 5am and thirty yards or so from the bedroom window of our Tuscan villa the Pavarotti of cockerels was giving us his rendition of Nessum Dorma.

The hills south of the mediaeval towers of San Gimignano were barely visible under the inky sparkling sky. The moon hung low in the west like a chunk of orange peel. Not even the early rising Italians were up at this unearthly hour. But I was.

Eventually I had convinced myself that the whole desert/vintage car/noisy horn thing was a demented dream from which I had to escape so I forced myself awake only to discover that the horrible horn was still screeching. Which I have to say was rather disappointing.

Normally when you manage to shake off a dream, say, if you're falling down a lift shaft and it turns into a journey to the centre of the earth, or if you're being buried alive by evil garden gnomes it's always comforting to know that when you awake you'll be Scot free.

Actually after this first bout with the cockerel I think I was more amazed than anything, principally at the bird's sheer brass neck, which I was already picturing myself wringing.

Even though we live in the country I have no first hand experience of cockerels, beyond the odd cartoon in which they persist on waking people up at the crack of dawn.

I had also never seen the crack of dawn, but here it was right in front of me just beginning to splinter along the distant eastern horizon. After failing miserably to con myself back to sleep I decided there was nothing for it but to get up and see what the cockerel was so excited about, but there was nothing much happening that I could make out.

My wife stirred and asked how my sore throat was doing.

The cockerel I reasoned was just doing his job, which is fine, but not on my holiday.

"What cockerel?" asked my wife four hours later over breakfast.

"The one that woke us up at five o'clock!" I declared, "The one that lives with the flipping chickens."

"Chickens?" she asked. "There's chickens?"

I knew there were chickens somewhere behind the Loggia – a sort of ancient roman playroom because I had heard them clucking. Or at least I had assumed they were chickens. I took my wife to meet them for a second opinion.

She gave out a long low whistle as she peered at them with her hands on her hips.
"Could be chickens." Was the best she could do.

I had to agree they were the strangest looking chickens I had ever encountered. They had huge flat heads and long stringy bald necks, as if someone had tried to strangle them and lost their bottle half way through. They also had big old feet, so maybe they had given their would be assailants the boot.

None of this was fooling me. I knew that somewhere inside that coop was a huge cockerel with an 80 fags a day habit. He was wisely keeping a low profile as I darted around trying to catch a glimpse of this mighty-throated bird.

Meanwhile the alien chickens strutted around pretending I had come to the wrong place. I obviously wasn't the first irate visitor who had been rudely awoken and turned up with menace on their mind.

Around lunchtime and again at teatime the cockerel let rip with a vengeance but after being baked in the Chianti sun everything as afar we could see was just lovely.

It was a different story around 5 am the next morning. I sat wide-eyed and bolt upright in bed followed rapidly by my wife as if we had been fired out of a big gun.

It may sound strange but after a few days of this we got into the swing of being mercilessly yanked out of a deep sleep and then dozing fitfully in a pool of sweat for a few hours while the sun scoured the bedroom like a massive searchlight. Anyway, we were only visitors, the cockerel didn't just live here, he was King.

Curiosity took me back time and again to the chicken coop. I knew I couldn't defeat the cockerel, I just wanted to see what I would have been up against if it had come to a clean fight.

Finally one scalding hot afternoon I spotted him perched on top of a stall of straw and I could hardly believe it. He was the smallest and loneliest looking rooster in all Tuscany, the Wizard of Oz of cockerels lording it over 14 females almost twice his size.

"He looks like he needs a good holiday." Scowled my wife, then she proposed taking him with us on our excursions. He would particularly have enjoyed a tour of the Chianti Communes, he was their logo, emblazoned much larger than life on all their signs and labels. But I don't think he would have travelled very well. Who knows what dangers he might have faced at the hands of a sleep deprived tourist.

Word must have got out that we had been sniffing round the chickens because the following day we were breakfasting – bleary-eyed on the most exquisite free eggs we had ever tasted.

We may have been bribed but we weren't deaf.

Up Close and Personal

I hate when people say to me, "Do you mind if I ask you a personal question'. Of course I mind, that's why they've asked me. The trouble is, you never know what's coming next. But you can be sure of one thing; you're going to be asked a question you really don't want to answer.

It depends of course on who's asking the personal question. For instance I suspect that most men would find an attractive blond in a slightly revealing dress difficult to turn away.

"That depends on how personal you want to get." Was my cheesy reply straight out of a bad movie and about half way down a bottle of Toscana Bianco.

The blond was staying in the apartment round the corner from us. In a whole week we had only exchanged a few pleasantries. She had discouraged us from visiting the supermarket down the hill because she didn't think it was up to much and sent us instead on a 25 kilometre round trip to a supermarket that was identical in every respect, expect that it wasn't called a Co-op.

However, since she and her equally tall and taciturn husband were leaving the following day she obviously decided it was safe to break cover and get up close and personal.

This didn't surprise me. Holiday neighbours often become best pals just prior to departure because they know they won't have to make an effort in the days to come. It's a bit like having a platonic one-night stand.

Having said that the blond took me completely by surprise. Probably because I didn't see her coming.

It was early evening and still very warm, about thirty degrees. I was sitting outside in the courtyard at my table writing, and my wife was inside preparing dinner. Our upstairs neighbour Martin was sitting at another table frowning over The Times crossword. Occasionally he would shout out a clue that he was stuck on and we would ponder it together.

There was a certain amount of wine and scenic beauty involved in this so as you can imagine I was fairly content until the blond popped up. I say 'popped up' quite literally because from the way she appeared at face level I reckon she must have been hiding under the table for some time, waiting for the right moment to launch her personal attack.

I wouldn't have minded but Martin had suddenly lost interest in his crossword and was now hanging on our every move. Like me he wanted to know just how personal she was going to get.

But the blond seemed in two minds, she stared at me and then flashed a glance at Martin, took a deep breath and fell silent. I had a feeling I was being played with. As the blond smiled and edged a little too close for comfort forcing me into a gentlemanly retreat I saw Martin, out of the corner of my eye, sitting upright to improve his view.

"Can you hear him making a noise in the early hours of the morning?" Asked the blond reasonably loudly. Martin and I both looked in the direction of the chicken coop.

Earlier we had been discussing the cockerel that woke us up every morning at five o'clock sharp. It lived about thirty yards away and we had been trying to work out how we could stretch that to thirty miles without the vineyard owners noticing. So far we had a half-baked plan involving a tape recorder which I related to the blond.

"Not the cockerel," she smiled strangely, "Him...and his family." I followed her nod and as I suspected it pointed at the chicken coop, except of course that Martin was sitting in the way.

Surely I thought she couldn't really be speaking about Martin while he was within earshot, but I'm afraid she was, and worse still, she didn't care, even though Martin was built like the chicken coop door.

The only thing I could of was the impromptu singing. Martin, his wife Jane and their two daughters sang a lot, in perfect sweet harmony. It was like being on holiday with the Von Trapps.

Never one to pass on a performance my wife had turned instantly into Julie Andrews and reduced me to my usual role of captive audience.

"They do requests you know." I said to the blond, in an attempt to defuse a potentially explosive situation.

"Do they?" she replied dryly, "Well do you think they know - how to stop waking us up in the middle of the night with all their thumping and banging about?"

Martin's eyebrows were now firmly planted on his hairline but I thought he was taking his new role of noisy neighbour from hell extremely well. Actually it was difficult to tell since he was opening his mouth and nothing but air was coming out. Maybe he was trying to serenade the blond but couldn't find the right words.

Meanwhile the attractive blond had turned decidedly sour on me and was now standing with her fists on her hips in full war council mode. And then Martin rose to his feet and copied her like a mirror.

A few minutes earlier I had been blissfully content almost beyond description and now I was a human fence stuck helplessly between two warring holidaymakers.

I almost felt like telling them they didn't know one another well enough to fall out but instead I thought I'd better stand up as well and at least try to stop them from going for each other's throats.

Thankfully Martin was quite happy for me to intercede on his behalf. Anyway I don't think he could believe his ears, and to be honest neither could I.

For a start I thought, Martin and his family's apartment wasn't above the blond's, it was directly above ours and as far as we were concerned they might as well not have been there. In fact for a family with two young girls and a baby boy they were remarkably and thoughtfully quiet. Apart from the singing of course, but that never happened at an unsociable hour.

So why was the blond and her family woken regularly in the middle of the night, and more to the point, even if she was, why bother mentioning it now when she was leaving the following morning? Either she was determined to start trouble or she thought Martin was deaf.

Unfortunately I said all this, but while the blond was trying to make a recovery it struck me that the Irish honeymoon couple were in the apartment above her.

"Wait a minute." I said, "Martin and his family aren't above you, it's the Irish honeymooners. They're probably just getting carried away, a bit too enthusiastic, experimental even, you know the sort of thing. Think of it as a blast from the past."

The blond paused for thought flaring her nostrils at me, flashed a false grin at Martin who was now fit to burst with laughter, then turned on her heel and swanned off.

According to Martin I had just got a little too personal.

Gummed

Apparently I've got some kind of gum infection, although I had to take my dentist's word for it as I left her surgery with a face like an old rubber tyre.

For the rest of the afternoon I was blissfully unaware of anything from the neck up – a not uncommon state of affairs these days I'm told. So for about four hours I had absolutely nothing wrong with me.

After filling a fledgling cavity for good measure the dentist had given me a prescription for antibiotics. The last time this happened I spent a week getting acquainted with every available toilet I could find, including one in a chip shop I just happened to be passing.

By the end of the antibiotic course I felt as if I had been hoovered out. So this time when the pharmacist handed over my prescription and asked in a loud stage whisper if I was prone to diarrhoea I had that familiar sinking feeling.

The queue behind me were anxious for an answer, an old lady stared at me with knowing sympathy.

"Not right now," I declared loudly, "But I presume I will be if I take these." I added, holding up the bag of antibiotics as evidence.

"Well, I'm sure you know the scout's motto." Smiled the pharmacist and moved on to the next customer.

On the way out I overheard a young girl ask her boyfriend what the scouts had to do with it, but I knew better and prepared myself for the worst by deciding right there and then that those antibiotics would never see the light of day.

A quick recce round the accompanying information leaflet confirmed my worst fears.

"You may have some side effects while you are taking your tablets..." it began in a worryingly casual tone and then as I suspected, proceeded to list a shocking catalogue of anguish and pain; headaches, sickness, drowsiness, gastro-intestinal upsets, weakness and possible numbness to extremities, a furred tongue, a nasty taste in the mouth and of course the inevitable itchy rash.

There was some good news. Only on rare occasions could the tablets cause muscle pain, lack of movement co-ordination, liver damage, blood disorders that may lead to anaemia, poor blood clotting and something really horrible called erythema multiforme.

I threw the packet into the glove compartment with a wide-eyed shudder, hoping I hadn't caught any of those side effects already, just by handling the box.

I considered this a lucky escape. For the moment, my face still felt as if it belonged to someone else, someone who might have had a mild gum infection but who certainly wasn't willing to exchange it for an ambulance load of ailments that were far worse. Which, unless I'm mistaken was basically the deal. I'd also forked out for this, but I thought a refund was taking the antibiotic backlash a little too far.

My wife agreed. She had spent a memorable week last time trying to communicate with me through toilet doors.

"See how you get on." She counselled. Which suited me to a tee.

What she meant of course was, just wait until the dentist's injection wears off and then you'll change your tune.

Happily, the thaw was a long time coming. Even by the following day I only had the after effect of the filling and the general unpleasant sensation of having had my teeth played like a piano.

It wasn't until later that evening when we were in the supermarket that I began to admit that there might be the remotest possibility of a gum infection. It still wasn't time for a press release but there was definitely something nagging the left side of my face.

When I checked myself in a mirror in the clothing department I discovered I could only smile with the right side of my face, while the left corner of my mouth insisted on drooping glumly downward. I pushed it up, but it just kept collapsing

"At least your only half grumpy." Consoled my wife as she weighed a handful of bananas.

There was also a small matter of the peculiar tingling inside my mouth, as if I had just chewed a strip of sandpaper, but I was keeping quiet about that. In fact I was scared to open my mouth.

Instead I went to the pharmacy section and after a lengthy perusal picked up a bottled of mouthwash specially designed to relieve gum infections and 'put that smile back on your face'.

Half an hour later we were still no nearer the check-out and I cracked. While my wife pondered over the contents of a freezer cabinet I sneaked the mouthwash out of the trolley and opened the box. It didn't exactly promise instant relief but there was no harm in trying.

Checking there was no one around I deftly unscrewed the cap and took a big swig of the horrible looking bright pink stuff just as my wife straightened up from the freezer.

Apparently she couldn't believe her eyes because she whipped out her specs and put them on for a second opinion.

"Apart from the fact that you haven't paid for that yet," she began, scolding me like a headmistress, "Where are you going to put it, because you can't swallow it!"

None of this had even crossed my mind and I just stared at her as if I was blowing an invisible trumpet. My mouth was also going rapidly numb so I looked anxiously round for somewhere to unload myself.

"Don't even think about!" warned my wife, "You'll just have to go to the toilet."

Unfortunately we were in one of those massive supermarkets and the toilets were about half a mile away at the other end. But there was nothing else for it; I would just have to make the journey past hundreds of shoppers looking like Dizzy Gillespie in full swing. Still, I reasoned, the chances of meeting someone I knew were slim.

Round the first corner I walked straight into Peter Watson, a former editor of this newspaper and a man I hold in the highest esteem. He hailed me with his usual cavalier style and slapped me playfully in the stomach.

The mouthwash went down in one gulp and I stood there with my weird half smile charting every millimetre of the vile liquid's descent down my gullet.

"You're looking very well!" declared Peter. No wonder, I thought, I had just disinfected my insides.

How I held a reasonably fluid conversation I'll never know. My mouth and throat were now completely numb and my tongue felt like a lump of old shoe leather. Peter probably thought I had been at the Gin.

When we parted company I turned to my wife for consolation.

"Do you think he noticed my stupid half smile?" I asked, sounding as if I was speaking through a glove.

"I think the bright pink lips probably diverted his attention." She replied flatly.

I kept my head down after that, weighing up a week on the loo against walking around like a gloomy transvestite with a speech impediment.

Civic Mindedness

The overhead streetlight at the end of the road had been on for weeks, which was just a waste of electricity as far as I was concerned. My wife agreed but couldn't raise the same level of enthusiasm. The chirpy chap on the council switchboard was suitably concerned and said he would get someone down to check it asap.

Then he asked for my address and phone number. I used to think this was so someone could phone you back or write to you and thank you for being so civic minded but its probably so they can add you to their database of nosy nothing better to do, small minded, annoying, waste of time callers.

"So you don't actually live in the street you're calling about?" asked the chap who was now slightly less chirpy.

"Does that matter?" I asked, "we're frequent visitors to your fine town and our civic mindedness travels with us wherever we go."

At least when I phone our local council they know who I am the moment I start speaking.

"How can we help you today Mr Phillips?" the receptionist will enquire brightly and I'll tell them about some rubbish that's lying around or a new hole in a road I've just driven into.

Last week it was a sinister buzzing noise coming from a green box in the pavement just round the corner from the local M&S store. I mentioned it to the manager but he said it was outwith his jurisdiction.

"Well it's not outside mine," I said and promptly reported it. The following day the buzzing had stopped. Job done.

"You'd better watch the council don't start thinking you're doing all this stuff yourself just so you can report it," said my wife, "littering by proxy I think they'd call it."

We were staring at the four wheelie bins that have been lying on the ground open for weeks in the garden of a house we often pass during our evening walk.

"Just ignore them," said my wife but I had already leapt over the low garden wall and was starting to get to grips with the errant bins. Two of them actually had rubbish inside them so someone was using them while they were lying on the ground.

Could have been an elderly person of course who couldn't pick the bins up.

"Oi, what do you think you're doing?" said a loud deep voice from behind me.

Looking up I found a bulky bald bloke in a black leather jacket glaring down at me. He looked puzzled, or perhaps he was just deep in thought and couldn't find his way out.

In fact he may have been trying to work out how far he could bounce me down the road. One thing's for sure it wasn't the sort of appreciative look you give someone who is doing you a favour.

Not that he needed it. He could have probably picked all four bins up at once and juggled them.

"Oh, I'm just picking these bins up, its all part of the service, are they yours by any chance?" I said smiling as I manoeuvred the last bin into place against the garden wall.

"Service?" said the bloke screwing up his face into a big red knot, "what service?"

"Neighbourhood Watch," shouted my wife.

"Neighbourhood Watch?" repeated the bloke glancing up and down the road.

"Yes, its all part of the Neighbourhood Watch friendly roadside assistance scheme," I said confidently as I pushed the last bin into place and dusted my hands together.

"What?" blurted the bloke looking around again.

For some reason he seemed to think I had accomplices and he was right but she was obviously now lying low somewhere while hopefully maintaining a hawk-like surveillance on proceedings.

"There we are, all nice and neat," I said with a broad smile, "now when a prowling burglar comes along, he or she, it could be a woman although I imagine house burgling is normally a manly pursuit, won't think your house is unoccupied, they'll think to themselves 'there's someone in that house because they're bins are very neat and tidy' and they'll move on looking for easier prey, that's how it works basically, anyway must dash, lots to do, good evening."

It was probably the length of my reply that stalled the bloke. Judging by his pained expression and complete silence it certainly gave him a lot to think about. Meanwhile I trotted smartly passed him and crossed the road.

He was still watching me as I hurried up the street. Passing a Neighbourhood Watch sign I suddenly felt quite pleased with myself. I was going to point out the sign to the bloke but when I looked round he was on his phone and then my wife appeared from behind a bush and joined me.

"If he's phoning the council he's out of luck," I said, "they closed three hours ago."

"I don't think he's phoning the council," said my wife looking back as we picked up the pace.

Oats in the Loft

You could comfortably house a family of four in our loft. They would have to be under five feet tall of course and the loft would have to be empty. I suspect there is an alternative set of house contents up there and for all I know there are doubles of my wife and I living amongst it.

This mysterious 'loft stuff' as its known, has travelled with us from house to house over the past thirty years. We're not even sure it's all ours, in fact I'm certain some of it isn't. Every house we've ever lived in has had stuff left in the loft, which we just kept and then moved to the next loft.

There's also a large collection of small pieces of old furniture we've attempted to restore or repair. They're too gruesome for the charity shop, yet they seem to possess some kind of potential future life.

I've often thought the loft would make a great office, although I'd have to stand with a permanent stoop. As I was reminded when I re-designed my forehead recently using a handy crossbeam.

I was hunting for a patchwork quilt my wife had decided she couldn't live without when I met the crossbeam full on. I'd been distracted by a large creepy doll hanging upside down.

Naturally I scowled at the crossbeam as I rubbed my throbbing head. Instead of apologising the crossbeam showed me a random pattern of small holes. For a moment I stared at them wondering how I had managed to produce such small holes with a single blow.

I didn't find the quilt so when I mentioned the holes in the beam my wife was doubly perturbed because it looked like we had a dubious infestation in the loft.

"We'll have to call in an expert," she announced, "we can't have holes in crossbeams in the loft, you never know where that could lead."

I'm reasonably certain my wife has no idea what a crossbeam is but I for one believed every word.

Half an hour later Gavin our pet joiner was on the phone talking about doing a recce. In a former life Gavin was a librarian and is a self-confessed expert on anything you like. His nickname used to be The Oracle but he's been digitally upgraded to 'Google'.

I think his pipe helps. It hasn't been lit for three years but it's always close to hand. He pointed it at the holes in the crossbeam while I shared my fantasy about replacing it.

"So was it a tornado?" asked Gavin looking round, "or did you just shake the house up and down and leave everything where it landed?"

I actually thought the loft was quite orderly but now I was seeing it through the eyes of a mega-librarian, I had to admit it was slightly random.

"You could probably house a family of four up here if it was tidy," said Gavin sucking pointlessly on his pipe, "how about some porridge?" he added.

It was just after ten on Saturday morning and I hadn't eaten myself, Porridge sounded like a plan.

Gavin opted for the original or 'unpoisoned' version as he called it while I'd plumped for the Blueberry – even healthier my wife had said.

"Do you want coffee with that?" asked my wife, "it's real."

"Not for me," said Gavin, "I've given up all artificial stimulants." He added sticking his unlit pipe back in his mouth as a harsh reminder. Then we had a lecture about wood boring insects. I tried to sneak off but Gavin was in the mood for action and off he went up the Ramsay ladder with his dainty pot of Porridge.

"Let's get this show on the road," he shouted. I looked at my wife and we both shrugged at one another.

Back up in the loft we stood for a moment silently staring at the boreholes in the beam, surveying them with our expert eye, or at least Gavin was, I just managed look as if I was staring knowingly. I've been in situations like this before with Gavin and I always have the overwhelming feeling that we're planning some kind of escape.

"What's the plan Major?" I asked.

Suddenly Gavin flipped his spoon round and dipped the wrong end into the porridge, scooping up a peanut's worth. I thought, if he's going to eat his porridge like that we'll be up here all day.

Instead he began pushing the porridge into the holes.

"An old carpenter showed me this trick," he said waving the spoon in front of him like a wand while blowing on the newly bunged up holes.

"I assume this old carpenter was sacked for devious practices?" I said.

"Actually he owned a multi-million pound company," replied Gavin.

I should have guessed. When the porridge dried there was no sign of the holes.

"It doesn't work so well with these fancy flavours," said Gavin pointing at the remains of my Blueberry porridge.

My wife was impressed, particularly as Gavin's consultation was free.

"Did you find the quilt?" she asked.

Champions

There's something about the sound of trumpets and drums that make the hairs on the back of my neck stand to attention and salute. It has to be mediaeval trumpets and drums of course, played on a warm Italian afternoon in the wake of several glasses of wine.

"A mediaeval battle!" I announced excitedly, waving the tourist information leaflet, "We must go to that."

My wife took the leaflet and frowned over it, possibly because it was in Italian.

I could already see this mediaeval battle in my head, a big live version of the plastic armies I used to line up on my bedroom floor. There would be knights in armour, pike men, blokes with crossbows, maces, broadswords, flags, plumed helmets the lot.

"Will it take long?" asked my wife, meaning of course, would the shops still be open when it was finished.

"Of course it won't take long," I laughed, "But it will be spectacular, apparently one half of the town fights the other, they've each got their own colours, big flags and stuff, it's an ancient feud."

"Sounds like a football match." She said, but we went anyway.

We'd been to Volterra before and it hailed ice cubes on us. This time the Etruscan hilltop town burned like an opal under the sun and big flags flapped high above us in the steep narrow streets like regimental washing.

In the courtyards and doorways lovely mediaeval babes and handsome hunks with long hair and tight hose were lurking like models waiting for a photoshoot. My wife was impressed, so it looked like fun for all the family.

Italians can be a posy lot at the best of times, but it was obvious that dressing up in this glamorous highly romantic period costume simply gave them a fresh excuse to let the world see how gorgeous they were. It was something they did naturally and I can't imagine any of them were getting paid for it.

Ahead of us a quartet of damsels and knights engaged in a noisy discussion fell silent as I focussed my camera on them. Lips were pouted and eyes smouldered for the lens. The girls meanwhile tossed their hair into black shining manes.

My wife told me not to encourage them, but I think it was too late. When I looked back they were still in the same pose.

Meanwhile up on the green plateau of the town park, under the Disney-like towers of the crenellated fortress, crowds of spectators were sorting themselves out around the grass arena.

A lot of people had decided to make a picnic out of it and judging by the amount of food and drink they had lugged up the cobbled hill, they looked as if they were settling in for the weekend. Tablecloths were being spread out and napkins tucked into necklines.

We gazed at these banquets forlornly, but by sheer fluke just a few minutes later walked straight into a bar hidden behind the fortress wall through a tiny overgrown archway.

We seemed to be the only tourists in the place and for once, we were the imposters.

The clientele was certainly remarkable, a surreal concoction of folk. Romeo and his lusty mates, complete with rapiers and bulging cod pieces were holding court at the bar, while under the shade of the pear trees nests of jolly old ladies, dressed as if it was VE day, gossiped and played cards.

Every few minutes an armoured warrior or a blousey wench would pop out of the archway in the wall as if they had been transported through a time portal. Two slightly amazed motorcycle policemen in sunglasses, boots and jodhpurs appeared as if they had come from the distant future.

On of the cops cadged a fag form Romeo and as they all mingled we felt like extras in a film studio waiting for our call.

When it came, it was by drum, a great primitive rumble that shook Romeo and his merry band into draining their glasses and making a run for it.

A young boy scampered back for the huge red and white flag he had left propped against the bar and the old ladies cheered and waved their cards at him.

We followed closely behind, aware that in the midst of this panoply and pageantry we had become satisfyingly invisible. So much so that we managed to pitch ourselves directly behind the PA control desk.

The big bearded courtier who was 'driving' the desk was perched on a wobbly melon crate. He'd also brought a picnic. He wasn't too worried about us standing beside his desk, but the baguettes were moved discreetly to a place of greater safety.

Suddenly the majestic procession of drummers and flag bearers appeared from under the fortress tower and the sunlit skyline became a flutter of silver, red, white and blue. Finally the trumpets turned up and that's when the hairs on the back of neck stood up.

When the knights and pikemen filed into the arena I was convinced some genetic switch had been thrown because I was ready to enlist. Once the two sides had assembled – the blue squiggles on the left, the red sunrays on the right, the flag throwers stepped out and started showing off, and showing off and showing off.

The first couple of times you see someone throw one of these enormous flags high above their head and wait for it to skewer them as it hurtles earthward, it is extremely impressive. The Italian appetite for such things, like all Italian appetites is boundless.

After an hour I was beginning to think I could do it myself. We had also realised why the veteran mediaeval battle fans had brought the contents of their kitchens with them.

Next up on the programme was a group of dancing maidens, a sort of 14th century Pan's People, or as the bloke from Manchester who was standing behind me announced, 'Eh up lads, tasty birds!'

The fact that they were dancing to an electronic gavotte by the 1970's pop legend Mike Oldfield in no way diminished their tasty birdness, but it sent my authenticity meter into orbit and broke the spell.

When battle finally commenced some two hours after the first drum roll, it was as I had promised my wife - very short and rather nasty. After a flurry from the archers and crossbowmen the two armoured sides clanked towards one another accompanied by heavy metal music and matched one another growl for growl until one side was hammered, quite literally to the ground.

"Blimey!" chuckled my Mancunian mate and then the music changed to 'We Are The Champions' by Queen.

Around the arena there were pockets of spectators heaving with laughing and everyone one of them I'm sure was British. As far as the rest of the Euro audience was concerned all that was needed now was a blast of the music from Gladiator and that would finish the day off nicely, which it did.

"Come on," said my wife, "If we hurry we can catch the shops before they shut."

Which we did.

The Magnificent Seven

Normally I hang about outside clothes shops like a bodyguard while my wife disappears inside for half an hour and tries on stuff she has no intention of buying.

I've tried accompanying her into these shops but sooner or later she gives me the slip and the next thing I know I'm the bloke lurking beside the lingerie.

No matter how disinterested he is in lingerie it's impossible for a man not to look guilty and break out into a suspicious flush when standing next to a display of black lace bras. It's certainly one way to attract the attention of women but it has no long term prospects.

So now I stand outside the shops at a safe distance and try not to look too much like a stalker. Although this isn't foolproof either.

A few weeks ago while I was loitering outside a busy women's clothes shop I was cornered by five members of my family whom I haven't seen for some time.

I was so amazed to meet so many of them at once – they were all out together on a big shopping trip, that I forgot to mention that my wife was inside the shop.

After about twenty minutes we said our goodbyes and I decided it was time to venture into the shop and remind my wife that there was an even more interesting life waiting for us beyond the shopping centre.

As I did so I had second thoughts, stopped and turned round to find the five members of my family staring at me in a huddle and all of them quite obviously convinced they had just uncovered my secret life as a closet cross-dresser. There was no point in trying to explain my way out of it, I just smiled and waved, but I was met with blank stares.

So last Saturday when my wife invited me to join her on one of her clothes shop forays I went with the flow. Either way I was going to end up looking like a spare part.

In any case she had promised she would only try on one jacket, although I didn't actually get it in writing. For some reason she thought I was joking and just laughed.

However, I thought this must be some jacket before my humble opinion was being sought, so if nothing else I was curious.

She had spotted this jacket on earlier recce, but apparently it had now been moved, or sold, or we were in the wrong shop and I had a blinding flash of deja vu. For a moment I saw us embarking on the great jacket hunt, plodding through shop after shop, round and round in ever expanding circles.

Fortunately my wife had a better idea and set off in search of an assistant.

While she was away I met an old friend – an Afghan jacket I hadn't seen for about 25 years. During that time it had succumbed to a slight makeover and acquired a faintly modern twist but it was still the Afghan jacket I had so many fond memories of.

"Have you seen this?" I laughed when my wife returned.

But obviously we weren't seeing the same thing. "Oh well done," she exclaimed, gripping my arm with excitement, "Clever you!"

She was absolutely overjoyed and of course so was I; in fact we seemed to be ecstatic.

This was great, I thought, if I'd known it would be this much fun I would have pointed out daft jackets before. But apparently it wasn't as daft as I thought because I had inadvertently found 'the jacket' and that wiped the grin off my face.

Before I had time to talk her out of it she had slipped off her own jacket and was sliding an arm into the decidedly dubious Afghan. I quickly looked around to make sure there was no one we knew about to pounce on us, and noticed we were more or less standing in the shop window. But when I tried to coerce my wife into a more secluded area behind some big winter coats she wouldn't hear of it and protested that she needed the light.

"So what do you think?" she asked, going through the unique repertoire of moves and flounces that women employ when they try on clothes in a shop, none of which will ever be repeated in the real world, except perhaps on a catwalk.

"Well," I began cautiously; knowing that I was entering a minefield that would inevitably be my undoing no matter which direction I took, so instead I ended up just nodding.

Eventually with some encouragement I decided the best I could do was, "It's very seventies," and braced myself for the impact.

"Exactly!" declared my wife. "It's just what I was looking for."

She then began rummaging in her bag and I watched with growing interest as she produced her camera.

"Right,' she said, with a certain focussed determination as she handed me the camera, "Two or three shots will do, it's got black and white film in it."

I stood there holding the camera under a worried half-smile as my wife assumed a pose. Frankly I was still trying to figure what difference the black and white film made. Either way I was going to look extremely dubious photographing my wife wearing an Afghan jacket in a busy shop right next to the window, although now I understood why she wanted the light.

"Come on," she said jolting me into action, "I don't want to be all day."

So I took her photograph, and another and another. When the flash went off it must have blinded half the shop, but at least it was cheaper than actually buying the jacket.

"What now?" I asked hopefully, "Lingerie shots?"

But she was back in her bag muttering something about a wig. Now we really were getting kinky.

Out came the longest blackest wig I have ever seen. My wife held it up and stroked her chin. "Maybe not." she said. We took one more shot for luck and the jacket went back on its hanger.

"We must do that again some time." I said and the next thing I knew I was covertly photographing birthday cards in the shop next door, only the cards with age 7 badges on them though, we were very particular. We also returned all the cards we had collected to their rightful place, well, almost.

Outside the shop I felt like an outlaw and my finger was twitching with excitement over the camera's button. My wife was delighted.

"Good," she said, "Come on, I need seven gloves and seven trouser legs."

"What about dwarves?" I suggested enthusiastically, but was told to keep it real.

We did manage to photograph seven hands however, which I was particularly proud of - the eighth hand was holding the camera.

I've learned one thing; there's definitely more fun to be had inside shops, all you need is an art project. Although if we carry on like this we're in serious danger of ending up on The South bank Show.

The Mind Reader

The strange thing was, an old autographed postcard of the diminutive magician Paul Daniels, just appeared from nowhere, dropping onto my desk like manna from heaven, face side up. It must have been sitting high up on a shelf and been blown off by a draught, but its arrival was nevertheless perfectly timed and rather spooky.

Daniels had presented the postcard to me to me with some aplomb after I had interviewed him. He said he wanted to give me something that would always remind me of the astonishing power of magic. The postcard features a grinning portrait of himself and his wife, the lovely leggy, former dancer Debbie Mcghee.

I stared at it and wondered what he would have made of the mysterious e-mail I had just received from a friend.

It was a PowerPoint file called The Mind Reader. Normally PowerPoint is used for creating animated presentations on your computer, I use it myself, but I'd never seen anything like this.

Although I must say I had opened the file with the scepticism I thought it deserved, probably because I'm a sucker for magic and I'm fed up being taken for a ride.

The Mind Reader looked especially dubious. For a start it said it was going to control my mind, which I thought would be a neat trick because even I can't do that.

After some preliminary waffle it presented me with a row of six playing cards and told me to select one, whisper it outloud and then click the mouse button to go to the next page.

"Blah, blah, blah.' I thought, but picked a card anyway, deciding at the last minute not to whisper it outloud – I was alone and I'm not that daft.

Smiling to myself I clicked the mouse button and up popped the row of cards again – with mine missing. After doing the biggest cartoon double take you can imagine I scrutinised the five cards, but the card I had picked – the black Jack of Clubs, had gone AWOL.

"Uh oh." I said, outloud - I thought it was justified, and went back to the start of the programme and picked another card. This time when my card was missing I jumped out of my seat. It was then that Mr Daniels' postcard fluttered grinning onto my desk.

Most people would have taken this as a supernatural omen, but most people haven't met Mr Daniels and I knew he simply wanted to get in on the act.

Since he had made such a spectacular entrance I decided to let him stay and watch. I think he would have been impressed because even after six or seven times my card was still missing and I wasn't amused anymore.

I was just worried, because the very fabric of my reality was been slowly shredded, revealing behind it a world of extraordinary possibilities, in otherwords - magic.

As far as the paranormal is concerned there's always safety in numbers, so when this sort of thing happens I find the best solution is to make it happen to someone else, as quickly as possible.

It was late and everyone in the office was packing up and going home, but I managed to find two willing victims.

"The Mind Reader...excellent..." they intoned, almost in unison with wide-eyed delight.

Suddenly all thoughts of home and the cosy hearth vanished as my two colleagues bent ever closer to the screen and were duly sucked in. This is what happens when intelligent adults spend too much time in the company of computers.

If the Mind Reader didn't work I was in real trouble. But of course it did, time and again every card that was picked was excluded mysteriously from the second row of cards.

"Right." whispered one of the computer experts, "This time we won't say the card outloud."

"Good idea," whispered the other one back, "I'll write it down."

If I hadn't thought of this myself earlier, I wouldn't have believed what I was hearing.

A card was pointed at in ritual silence then scribbled on a piece of paper, which was folded and slipped quickly into a back pocket.

"Could be a hidden camera." Explained my furtive colleague, but I wasn't saying anything.

When the Mind Reader came up trumps again I left my mystified victims arguing about whether the computer had a built-in microphone.

I felt much better now, but in the car on the way home I was still haunted by rows and rows of sniggering playing cards that looked suspiciously like Paul Daniels.

But unknown to me Paul must have been working his magic because in a blinding flash it suddenly struck me how the Mind Reader worked.

Once again I was the Master and I toyed with the idea of turning back and revealing the secret to my poor frenzied colleagues, but I decided to leave them revelling in the realm of the paranormal for the moment. Even though I was slightly envious.

This was the downside of deciphering the Mind Reader - I had burst my balloon and had a bit of a wobbly lip on. I needed a fresh victim to cheer myself up. Admittedly my father-in-law Ian was a soft target, but he would do for practice.

"Pick any card," I said, gesturing with a magician's flourish at the row of cards.

"What for?" he asked, his face eerily lit by the screen of my laptop. This was obviously going to be more difficult than I thought.

"Just do what you're told!" I barked, so he muttered into the screen and made a reluctant selection.

"Right, which card did you pick? I asked, but he wouldn't tell me, in fact he was outraged that I should take him for such a mug.

It made no difference, I thought, and when I clicked the mouse button and the second row of cards came up I just stood there trying not to look too smug as I waited for his gasp of amazement, but nothing happened.

"Amazing eh?" I prompted.

"What's amazing about that, my card's still there," he replied pointing at the screen.

I couldn't believe this was happening, so I started the programme again and demanded that Ian pick another card, which he did after some encouragement.

"Still there," he said with grim confidence.

Now I was getting annoyed. So we tried it again and again but for some reason Ian's card refused to budge. The Mind Reader it seemed had a mind of its own.

"Aye, you'll have to do better than that," advised Ian lighting his pipe as I closed my laptop with a beaten, hangdog sigh.

I didn't tell Ian that it was impossible for the Mind Reader to fail because the first row of cards was completely different from the second. So no matter which card was picked from the first row it would always be missing from the second.

I couldn't make up my mind whether I had been outmatched or not, but I imagine Paul Daniels doesn't have an autographed postcard of me on a shelf in his office.

Home Comforts

You would think that a sweet painting of three cute puppies would brighten up even the dourest of places, perhaps bring a scrap of home comfort to an otherwise cold unrelenting environment. But those little puppies weren't fooling me. Confidently sinister was how I described them, to myself of course.

I'd shuddered when I saw them; hanging above the stony stairway as if they were guarding the mysterious dimly lit upper floor. Someone had probably put them there thinking they would brighten the place up, but I could hear the theme music from The Omen. At least they weren't kittens.

"What a great place!" I announced enthusiastically.

"Yeah, great," agreed my son Adam; "It's even got puppies, pity they're not kittens."

"Never mind, look its got...fire extinguishers." I struggled helpfully. My wife shot me a black look, but it was all I could come up with.

"And there's a payphone!" shouted Adam. My wife nudged me, as if to ask why I hadn't spotted that. Adam dropped his mobile phone a few weeks ago and it didn't bounce back so the world is now one annoying digital ring less.

"I wouldn't get too excited about that, I bet there's normally a huge queue for it." I warned, despite the fact that the three of us were standing in an empty hallway staring at a lonely payphone.

My wife thought I was possibly confusing the nurses' home with a prison, but I wasn't, I couldn't see much difference.

But this was Adam's first taste of hospital accommodation and probably because he didn't know any better, he liked it. To be fair I think he was seeing a different place from us because he was smiling and gazing into the distance. Perhaps into the future where all manner of wonderful things would be happening around him.

Décor or the lack of it seemed to be the last thing on his mind. As far as he was concerned he had arrived at party central and a great rolling social life was thundering towards him like an all-engulfing tidal wave of fun.

"Must be dozens of nurses here, dozens..." He mused, mouth open, as he scanned the floor above us.

Adam would only be spending a month training at the cottage hospital but it was obvious his social calendar was already filling up.

He wasn't exactly rubbing his hands as we climbed the green stony stairs, he was too laden with bags, but he had such great expectations written all over his face that I was seriously thinking about paying him the odd visit - see if he wanted any odd jobs done, fatherly advice, that sort of thing.

As we passed the puppies I noticed that one of them was snarling.

"Oh look!" shouted Adam smiling; "Here's a photograph of their dad."

Sure enough there was a small framed photograph above me of an even bigger snarling dog. Whatever was up here needed some serious protection.

"Aw, he's great." Enthused Adam screwing up his face with delight.

Adam likes animals, he should have been a vet but then he would have missed out on this place.

It looked like the sort of Spartan public baths you would find in Bulgaria, drained of course. Although it was scrupulously clean, but then so are morgues and it was definitely big on fire extinguishers.

Along the gloomy corridor we passed a deserted arid little lounge that had been based on the set of Rising Damp, but without the laughs.

"Very nice." I said nodding in the doorway. At least the TV worked. I half expected the Bulgarian weightlifting championships to be on, but it was Heartbeat playing a Freddie and The Dreamers song while a reclusive farmer had a nervous breakdown because his wife had run off with his prize ferret. Somehow it all seemed very apt.

The hospital was certainly far from the madding crowd, or at least the madding crowd that's in a position to pay for entertainment.

"I bet there's a big argument every night over the telly," I reflected. But I could see Adam was already on another channel that was slightly more interactive.

His room was just about big enough to swing that prize ferret, but there was a large mirror so that was a relief. You have to look your best when there's fun on the cards.

Although so far we hadn't seen another living soul.

"You'd think there would be a porter or a caretaker." Said my wife, "Or even a shade for the table lamp" I added.

"It's not The Shining." Laughed Adam. But I wasn't so sure; The Overlook Hotel had already crossed my mind.

Food must have crossed Adam's so we went in search of the kitchen. Although first we went in search of the light switches because so far we had been fingering our way along the corridors by cold moonlight, which in hindsight had added a certain glamour.

None of the doors we passed said 'Kitchen' so I began opening them; tentatively I might add, remembering I was in a nurses' Home and not Carry on Nurse.

The tiny kitchen turned out to be quite close which put a big smile on Adam's face. But it didn't stay long when he realised he had forgotten to bring something very important.

"Food?" I asked, but it wasn't that serious, just the alarm clock that would wake Adam at six o' clock the next morning in time for his first slice of life on a hospital ward.

This was the notorious alarm clock Adam normally carries with him everywhere, in lieu of a watch. It's the alarm clock that went off and couldn't be switched off during a lecture and in a packed theatre during a silent contemporary dance performance, forcing the old gent in his cravat across the aisle from me to sit bolt upright and salute. It was also the alarm clock that went off in the car all the way to Edinburgh because we couldn't find it hidden in the boot.

So now we set off to find someone who could lend Adam an alarm clock for the night. Reluctantly the three of us split up and went in different directions covering both floors of the distinctly eerie Home. As we tapped warily on doors and fell accidentally into broom cupboards it was like being in Scooby Doo.

Ten minutes later when we all met back in the central hallway we gave one another an enormous fright and shouted in unison, "There's no one else here!"

Adam decided everyone was over in the hospital, but I had a feeling they weren't, because no one in their right mind would live in an overheated drained swimming pool.

Adam made arrangements for a nurse to wake him the next day – porridge, a round of toast, coffee, a thick ear.

The next day he walked into the village to buy a travel alarm clock and the following morning was woken at four o'clock by a big nasty fickle old clock ringing in the bottom drawer of his dresser. At least he's not completely alone.

Five Items or Less is More

There's nothing better than having an argument by proxy, you can say what you like and get boiled up without fear of reprisals.

Even from a distance I could tell my wife had been in a fray. In fact she'd just been in Marks & Spencer but she was carrying more than a bag of messages. Although she seemed to be smiling her post-battle trauma was all over her like an ominous cloud of fall-out.

"Two things." She had promised, "That's all I'm going in for."

So I circled the busy streets like a hawk but after half an hour I started looking for somewhere to park, or rather somewhere to hide from the real hawks, the traffic wardens.

I was lucky; a genial traffic warden caught me with a disapproving smile. So I saluted and drove off. It was easy for both of us.

My wife had not been so fortunate. To anyone else she would have probably seemed perfectly calm when she got into the car, she was definitely smiling, but I knew it was a distant half-smile that had nothing to do with me.

My mother sometimes had this smile and I knew what was coming next, in fact I was almost looking forward to it.

"Go on then," I said, "What happened?"

Normally my wife would play hard to get, pretend nothing had happened, crank up the tension until one of us cracked. But this time there was no holding back and she began to seethe, so I began to seethe.

As I had suspected, those two items had turned into ten. But there was worse to come because my wife had gone to a five items or less checkout in the mistaken belief that it was designated for car collection.

This was all I had to hear. "And you got a row from the checkout girl." I said flatly.

"No, listen," my wife said confidentially, as if she were about to divulge a great secret, "I got a row from the woman behind me in the queue."

It's just as well we were sitting at a red light, because I think I would have driven straight into the car in front I was so mad.

"Don't get too excited yet," warned my wife, "You haven't heard the half of it."

But it was too late and I could already feel my blood pressure starting to rise. I hadn't even heard the story and I was ready to go back to the shop and give this other woman in the queue a piece of my mind.

"Right," I said, "Start form the beginning, I want all the facts." Which was a lie, I just wanted to relish every moment.

I believed my wife when she said she mistakenly joined the wrong checkout queue, this didn't surprise me. When she realised what she had done she apologised to the checkout girl profusely and then offered to join another queue. But the girl just smiled and explained that it was company policy to let customers through who had exceeded the five items limit.

You can understand this, it's a shop after all and they want to sell things. So my wife thanked her for being understanding and relaxed.

Unfortunately the woman behind my wife wasn't in the same frame of mind.

My wife said she sensed something was wrong long before the woman said anything. The hairs on the back of her neck stood to attention and she felt inexplicably uncomfortable. She had entered a primal state of fight or flight and all she was doing was buying a few messages.

Then someone tutted loudly behind her, but my wife ignored it, thinking it had nothing to do with her. But then they tutted again even louder and followed it up with a few 'disgracefuls' and a terse 'some people honestly', loud enough for the people in the next checkout to hear.

When the rest of the queue began muttering darkly my wife realised that she was the 'some people' who were being 'disgraceful'. My wife glanced round in time to see a middle-aged woman directly behind her mobilising the growing chorus of disapproval into a posse.

My wife satisfied most of them with an apology and a smile, but the woman marshalled herself for a head on confrontation. Again my wife apologised and explained how she had offered to move but the checkout girl had said it was all right. She was almost finished anyway so she had barely held anyone up.

"Well, sorry's not good enough!" Said the woman curtly.

"I beg your pardon?" replied my wife, starting to warm up nicely.

"You heard me sorry's not good enough!" persisted the woman loudly.

Trying to stay calm my wife explained in detail how she thought she had been standing at the checkout for car collection, but the woman wasn't interested in feeble excuses.

"Well you're evidently not standing in the car collection checkout are you. Can't you read or something." She barked.

When I heard this I ducked. If the woman had any sense she would have done the same.

"Tell me," my wife began, literally seeing red as she squared up to the woman, "Is it your hobby to stand behind people in queues and tell them off when they've bought too much stuff. You're the queue traffic warden, breathing down the back of people's necks and giving them rows!"

I really wish I'd seen this, but I probably would have done what everyone else was doing around the pair of them, trying to look invisible while straining to hear every word. Quite honestly Marks & Spencer has rarely been so exciting.

The checkout girl meanwhile was doing her best to calm things down, but the woman wanted her pound of flesh and began shouting for a supervisor, then the manager.

By this time my wife's messages were packed and she had paid for them but the checkout had come to a complete standstill and people were avoiding what must have looked like a set-up for You've Been Framed.

A homely Supervisor bustled up and my wife pitched in first with her side of the story. But the irate woman just thought my wife was making a confession and demanded to know what the supervisor was going to do about it - perhaps a custodial sentence was too much to hope for, but a life ban from the shop would do.

My wife was more interested in protecting the checkout girl whom the woman had threatened to report.

When the supervisor took the same stance as the checkout girl the action went from bad to ridiculous. My wife left while the woman demanded to know everyone's name.

After hearing all this I was less enthralled than I had expected. I was just scared. When we stopped at the next set of traffic lights an angry middle-aged woman frowned darkly at the car.

"Don't worry champ," Said my wife reading my nervous look. "That's not her."

Thank goodness for that, I thought. As I said, there's nothing better than a second hand argument.

The Middle-Earther

Personally I thought my cold was coming on a treat. After a week of being vaguely under the weather, which I could almost ignore, I progressed to being not quite a hundred percent. Although in my case this could of course be an all year round kind of thing, which several people were quite happy to point out.

The trouble was, I just wasn't in the mood for a cold. I had too much to do and didn't feel I could really devote enough time and attention to it. Obviously it's the season for sniffles and everyone has to do their bit, but I thought I'd given rather generously last month with that weird dizzy flu-type thing.

It was a strange one. It ambushed me one night as I lay down in bed. The moment my head hit the pillow the whole room turned into a carnival ride. I once jumped onto a waterbed that wasn't properly filled up and it was a similar experience.

But you don't expect to bob around in your own bed like a floating cork, not involuntarily. During the night I really did seem to toss and turn without moving a muscle. At one point I convinced myself I had fallen out of bed and made such a noise I woke my wife.

She peered at me wrapped snugly inside my duvet nest as I apologised for having fallen on the floor, then baffled and highly bemused she went back to sleep.

Over the next few days this fairground effect became known as 'that woozy feeling'. Every so often I would be hijacked and swept along on one of those old funfair rides where the floor came alive suddenly and tried to tip you over.

This was swiftly followed by general flu-type symptoms, just in time in fact to stop me from declaring I had a brain tumour and diving into a trembling panic.

"I told you it was nothing serious." Comforted my wife as I lay there half-delirious and racked with aches and pains.

So this little cold I had picked up was nothing I couldn't handle. After a few days my head was completely bunged up and then for no apparent reason it turn into a giant tap which I couldn't turn off. Plumbing has never been my strong point.

But it must have got fed up, because it stopped streaming as abruptly as it had begun. Then I settled down to the usual uphill struggle towards relative normality.

My wife had told me that some scientists think that women live longer than men because they wash their hands all the time, so that was me more or less installed in the bathroom with a range of antiseptic soaps.

Maybe it's something you have to work at because it didn't quite have the immediate effect I was looking for. Bang on time for the weekend my cold made an impressive comeback.

My father-in-law Ian however, wasn't so sure when he phoned to cheer me up.

"Doesn't sound like an ordinary cold to me." He intoned gravely, "Sounds like something far more serious and deadly."

He forgot to add, 'aye, yer doomed laddie, doomed' but it had a similar effect.

"Rubbish," I croaked, then coughed and spluttered for about a minute, "It's just a cold, I feel much better already."

Just as well I was sitting down or I think I would have fallen over, but I knew a cold when I had one.

To prove my point I took my cold out for a long crisp winter walk down a damp riverbank before calling in to see Ian. The idea was that the long crisp winter walk would work like a charm on my blocked tubes and break up my cold – again.

Instead, my tubes stayed stubbornly shut and I broke up instead. On the way back up the hill the gravitational force seemed to be particularly powerful and wanted to pull me down head-first on a journey to the centre of the earth.

"Look if you feel faint just say so." Announced my wife.

I took some time to get up that hill - my wife looked at her watch twice and as I flopped utterly exhausted into the nearest armchair, feeling reasonably sorry for myself, Ian stared hard at me. Here it comes, I thought, the gloomy diagnosis from Doctor Dread.

"Aye, well you've certainly put on weight since I last saw you." He pronounced and then sat back in his chair, his medical work finished for the day.

I couldn't remember stuffing my face with any enthusiasm since I last saw Ian two weeks earlier and I politely told him as much.

"Well, your face certainly looks fatter to me." He replied matter of factly.

And that was it. I didn't have a cold but I had a fat face. If that was meant to cheer me up it wasn't working. Personally I would have preferred some sympathy. But what I really needed was antibiotics.

The following morning I managed to get an emergency appointment with my GP so I could show her my fat face. There had also been a series of developments during the night. Apart from my face getting even fatter, my head felt like an old football, my ears felt like giant bags of fluff and my right eye had obviously tried to jump out of its socket when it saw its red-ringed self in the mirror.

I gave the Doc the whole story from the beginning, right back to the first flying bed incident, through all the woozy stuff and now the fat face and the big pop-eye.

She looked at me satisfyingly concerned and I thought, at last, someone who understands me. In order to do that however, she had to take my blood pressure, which turned out to be a little high, which was definitely a first. Then she had a look in my right ear, scribbled some notes and sat back playing with her pen.

"So, do you drink much...alcohol I mean?" she asked.

I told the truth. I'm a moderate drinker, no beer, no red wine, no spirits, apart from a little gin, and no liqueurs. Basically I don't drink anything but dry Martinis and I never drink during the day.

She stared at me in silence, frowning intently.

Wait a minute, I thought, fat face, feeling woozy, high blood pressure, big pop-eye and alcohol. Even I could add up that sum. The Doc had me down as a boozer.

I was about to protest my temperance when she explained that I had a viral infection of the middle-ear, my sinuses were obviously severely blocked and that alcohol would make them worse. Which was still bad news.

Back home as I spun rings around myself my wife said I looked like a bad special effect. Perhaps, she added I really had an infection of the middle-earth and the pain and facial swelling, the general disorientation with reality was merely part of my transformation. Imagine a horrible moaning extremely sober squashed Hobbit writing this and you'll get some idea of what she means.

Ratty

We could have been strolling through the set of one of those TV period dramas that always starts with a horse drawn carriage bowling confidently across the screen. The lighting department had certainly done a great job conjuring up an evening that was positively gothic, yet surprisingly comforting.

"It's very authentic isn't it," I said, meaning I suppose that the scene lived up to my expectations of what a street that was hundreds of years old should look like on a damp wintry night.

At the end of the narrow ancient street crouched the vague form of an even older Cathedral, its twin spires sprouting like horns and turning the building I imagined into a giant Minotaur, but I thought I would keep that allusion to myself.

"Well of course it's authentic." said my wife suddenly. She had been ruminating for a minute or so, trying to work out if I was being profound, or just profoundly stupid.

She was right of course. Carriages really had rumbled over these cobbles ferrying Bishops and finely dressed gentlefolk back and forth between the town and the large elegant houses that had grown up like an elite club around the Cathedral.

Most of these grand mansions remain enviably impressive, although there is always the consolation that some of them have fallen on hard times.

"Just as I thought," I'll say to my wife conspiratorially, "flats." And she'll nod knowingly at the stack of doorbells and nameplates.

Even better are the 'student flats', so good in fact that they are only ever mentioned in a stage whisper. Fortunately these are easy to spot, because as a rule they have at least one fully lit large room with no curtains or blinds, ensuring an excellent view of a torn Matrix movie poster on the far wall, a mountain bike turned upside down on the dining table and a window sill lined with empty beer bottles.

We always say this is a horrible state of affairs while secretly thinking it looks like brilliant fun for the tenants – living in such splendid faded grandeur without the financial albatross it takes to prop it up.

"This is my favourite." remarked my wife wistfully as we approached a particularly well maintained Georgian house with big black iron gates and only one name on the door.

Through what I assume would have been the original withdrawing room window we could see a smart dinner party in full swing. One of the men was wearing a cravat and looked remarkably like the Duke of Edinburgh.

"Spare a crust for a pair a'poor orphans guvnor!" I said loudly and was immediately ushered on with a lecture about inverted snobbery. We were laughing then but just a few yards on the street dipped suddenly into an unsettling gloom and we were in Dr Jeckyll and Mr Hyde territory. Under the pools of light the cobbled street gleamed like crocodile skin.

"Could be a setting for a Sherlock Holmes mystery - at a push." I suggested hopefully, but there was no mistaking the fact that the darkness seemed to be closing in on us like a cloak.

"Anybody could jump out on us here and we'd be none the wiser." Whispered my wife. Presumably she was whispering so as not to alert any potential ambushers.

No sooner had she said that than a small black cat ran out in front of us. If my wife had believed for one minute I would have caught her she would have leapt into my arms, but I was too busy pinning myself to a horrible clammy wall.

The little cat stopped in the middle of the road and ran back towards us, somehow managing to make itself smaller.

"It's only a kitten," I shouted laughing. But it wasn't.

As it changed its mind and course it hurried down the street ahead of us like a clockwork toy. We watched with growing curiosity until it stopped under a street light and revealed its true identity.

"Oh my God it's a rat!" I shouted.

"How do you know it's a rat?" my wife shouted back, grabbing my arm.

She had a point. Even though we live in the country I've never seen a rat in my life; in fact my entire knowledge of rats is limited to one shining example.

"Tales From The Riverbank?" exclaimed my wife.

I quietly reminded her about Roderick the Rat and my life of playground hell but she wasn't convinced.

"Maybe it's escaped from one of the houses." She suggested, staring hard at the dark shape sniffing hopefully along the gutter on the opposite side of the road.

"Maybe we should catch it and take it back to its owners," I said, following her stare, "There might be a reward. We could just knock on all the doors and ask people if they've lost a rat."

"Could be a gerbil, or a hamster." Said my wife tugging at her chin for inspiration.

"With a long leathery tail?" I asked.

Right on cue, Ratty darted out of the gutter and scuttled across the road and up onto the pavement about five or six yards in front of us. My wife shuddered visibly when she saw that long leathery tale for herself.

I suggested we keep walking since Ratty seemed quite happy to go about his business without attacking us. So as we continued down the dimly lit damp street it would have looked to anyone gazing out of their window as if we were taking a rat for a walk.

"Please, an R-A-T." corrected my wife. Which interested me. After living with these fellow mammals for thousands of years some people still can't bear to say their name.

Suddenly my wife had a revelation. We had just passed the University Zoological Department from where Ratty had obviously escaped.

"He's probably vital to their research," she declared, "let's help him escape."

"He has escaped," I replied.

"Well maybe he's lost," said my wife.

At this point Ratty bolted at a ninety-degree angle, hunkered down in the middle of the road and gazed back at us. In the gloom he looked like a big fat cobble that had been knocked out of place, except of course that he was breathing heavily.

I had to help my wife past what she called 'the line of fear' and so we tiptoed in complete silence as far as we could as if we were escaping from a dozing ogre. Round the corner with the Cathedral graveyard looming over the wall a brisk run was suddenly in order.

Back home on my laptop I typed Rat into the Internet search engine and a few seconds later there he was staring back at me.

"Yes, that's him!" agreed my wife like a witness in a police line-up. "What's his form?"

"Rattus norvegicus," I read, " Often referred to as the Fancy Rat."

"So I was right," she said smiling smugly. I frowned at her baffled. "How do you figure that out?" I asked.

 "Fancy Rat," she pointed, "I told you he was special, in fact positively posh."

Moving Time

My mother once moved house and forgot to tell my father. He was at sea, or rather an ocean at the time, on the other side of the world so my mother had a watertight alibi and about three months to pull the whole thing off. Which she did with her usual quiet determination.

We didn't move very far, less than two miles down the road, but it would have been a move too far for my father. You can see his point; he spent half his life on a house that moved around all the time.

Once we were firmly ensconced in our new home my mother sent my father a telegram but somewhere along the line of ports it missed him.

One afternoon the new occupants of our old house came home and discovered they had been burgled by an irate naval officer who couldn't find the biscuits – he hadn't got passed the kitchen.

Years later when I asked him what he made of that incident my father just shrugged his shoulders – while eating a biscuit and said worse things happen at sea.

Which I think was a typically male response. He would have put up a fight about moving house, but once it was all done and dusted and the removal men had come and gone and the carpets were down and the wallpaper was up he was perfectly happy with the situation, in fact he didn't even mind coming home to a house full of complete strangers.

Worse still, before tracking us down, he went for a game of golf – because it was such a nice day.

If I'm going to be so lucky I'll have to join the navy quick.

It was definitely an escape route I was looking for when I arrived home last week and discovered a For Sale sign outside our Steading.

Even although I was half expecting it, seeing the For Sale sign for the first time standing proud like a frozen defiant flag at the entrance to our drive was like slamming into a brick wall.

I might as well have done, because I braked so sharply, I almost gave myself whiplash.

"So what did you think when you saw the sign?" asked my wife on the phone. She was obviously excited

I couldn't think of a fib fast enough so I just told her the truth - that I jumped out of the car, pulled the sign out of the ground, started to throw it into the nearby burn, came to my senses at the last minute and stuck the sign back in a more prominent position.

She was relieved and congratulated me, until I added that I had painted a big white questionmark after the words 'For Sale'.

"I was going to write, 'maybe' above 'For Sale', but the questionmark was easier." I continued matter of factly. "More to the point."

She went silent, but she did laugh in the end, nervously.

The debate about whether or not to sell our Steading and move to a smaller house has been brewing since the servants escaped, or, as we prefer to think of it, our sons moved out. The same thing happened to James Stewart in the film Shenandoah, but he went and got most of them back.

"Just wait until your children leave home." Everyone said, "Then you'll have the place all to yourselves, it'll be bliss."

Which is true if you live in a modest sized house, but with a place the size of ours it's like running a cruise ship with no crew and no passengers.

"Lodgers!" my wife announced one day, "That's what we need, we'll turn the Steading into a B&B."

Knowing this was never going to happen but that the very thought of it would send me screaming for cover, she persisted with this sadistic fantasy and after just ten minutes had the upper floor of the house filled with improbably tidy natural history students who would turns our gardens into a field study.

Hotel management students were added as an afterthought, apparently they could run the house while we were engaged in matters of a more cerebral nature.

A few weeks later my wife had another unsettling brainwave. The Steading already resembles an art gallery so why not make a business out if it, we could sell our own work from the comfort of our own home.

Better still we could convert some of the rooms into a coffee shop or even a small restaurant and then convince Channel 4 to make a documentary about how much of a mess we made of it.

"Think of the column inches you would get out of that." She enthused, her eyes widening and glinting with a worrying madness.

All of which sounded too much like hard work and I had a creeping feeling I was being corralled like an unruly sheep towards that For Sale sign. I knew what my father would have done, but unfortunately I don't play golf.

The property girl who came round to value the Steading agreed.

"Far easier just to sell." She said nodding comfortingly, "And move to something smaller."

But I think she just said that because she had her eye on the place for herself.

After we had shown her round and told her all the things we had done to the Steading over the past seven years, my wife and I were left sitting like proud smiling parents at our offspring's graduation ceremony. But it didn't last long.

Half an hour later my wife had the camera out.

"Mementoes?" I asked, trying to look like a poor homeless orphan cast out into a storm.

"Don't be daft." She laughed, "We'll need photographs for the schedule."
You can't begin to imagine the effect that word schedule had. My wife only said it once but she may as well have slapped me on the back of the head with a bucket full of schedules.

Time for a new tack I thought as I stumbled around reeling from the aftershock.

"It's a shame we'll have to sell most of our furniture," I said later.

My wife scratched her head and thought about this for a moment. I felt sure I had dropped a whopping great depth charge and waited for the explosion.

"Well, hopefully we can sell some of it with the house," she said finally.

The furniture was my best shot. Some pieces took months to find and months to restore. They are cherished and guarded like the family jewels and now my wife was willing to flog them off to the first person that took a fancy to them.

"What's wrong now? She asked frowning, "it's only stuff, it's only a house, home is where the heart is."

I said all this as I planted the For Sale sign back in the ground and felt much better for it. Although it's still an unsettling feeling seeing that sign. Every time I arrive home I think, 'oh that's funny, someone's put our house up for sale, what a cheek!'

I imagine it's a similar experience to being tattooed, painful but at the same time exciting with the hope that it's all going to be worth it in the end.

Clutter

It might seem a sad admission but in our house when the cat's away the mice clean out cupboards, and drawers, chests and trunks, the shed, the loft, the pend.

Anywhere in fact that has lain untouched by the hand of logic.

The first thing I did when my wife left for a week in Holland was rush out and buy our new home before she had even seen it. The second thing wasn't quite as exciting but was just as therapeutic.

I was writing in the dining room where my wife usually works, surrounded by stuff, when it occurred to me that now was my chance to clear out our clutter.

Normally when I throw stuff out my wife ambushes the wheelie bin and rescues all the junk she claims I've dumped indiscriminately. This is a slight exaggeration on her part.

She says I can't just chuck things out without examining them properly. But I always make a point of at least scanning the top of the pile of rubbish before consigning it to the bin. I find the deeper you dig the more interested you become, and that's fatal.

So anyway the same old rubbish has been coming back to haunt us for years. It's constantly mixed in with the new stuff so in a way I suppose we do practice a form of recycling.

From an archaeological point of view this would make dating our clutter practically impossible. As far as building a picture of its owners, I hate to think what they would come up with.

It would be fairly obvious that we worshipped broken things, perhaps in the belief that one day they would magically repair themselves and that we revered odd strands of wool, tangles of horrible string, unidentifiable pieces of rock and photographs of complete strangers – and their pets.

Everyone thinks they hoard junk in the hope that it will 'come in handy' but there's not much you can do with seven years worth of Christmas cards. Unless you give them back to the people that sent them so they can save some money by sending them to you again.

I suppose if everyone did the same we could eventually bring the Greeting Cards industry to a halt.

However I am yet to be convinced by the prospective handiness of half a nutcracker.

I suspect our inclination to store unnecessary rubbish stems from our innate reverence for objects. Basically it's a form of animism.

The same instinct that makes us throw coins into fountains and pools prevents us from chucking out a broken camera with no lens. So we daily fill the spaces around us with things, like a wall, or to be more exact like a protecting veil.

That's the problem with moving house, it's difficult to justify moving that security blanket of junk, particularly if you have to pay someone to do it.

Which explains why I was rubbing my hands with sinister glee when I realised the bin men would have been and gone before my wife got back. Even better - our neighbours were away and I could hijack their wheelie bin to the cause.

The thought of being able to fill two giant bins with rubbish was almost too much and I had to sit down for a few moments and marshal my thoughts, devise a plan

The stove was on, blazing away, so I could burn the three thousand Christmas cards and the photographs of complete strangers and their attendant pets.

I could also burn the duff photographs my wife took with her thumb over the lens. There were at least fifteen years worth of them – vague faded forms threatened by an approaching giant pink blob.

"You can't throw them out!" my wife always pleads, "That's us sailing up Loch Katrine onboard the Sir Walter Scott, and that's my thumb."

Strangely when I threw the bundles of blurred and bleached snapshots into the fiery furnace I couldn't bare to watch them shrivel and catch light. For some reason the Christmas cards were worse, in fact it was a slightly traumatic experience. So I opened the vent and they went up like a Roman Candle.

All those bits of string and wool went the same way. The collection of bus and train tickets I hovered over momentarily, convinced that someone might part with real money for a complete set of Bluebird bus routes.

But in the end they made a fine blaze and after half an hour I had to strip down to my T-shirt and shorts.

There were items that flummoxed me completely. Like the set of denture impressions, not quite someone else's teeth but the gruesome next best thing. I held them up to my face in front of the dresser mirror but they were far too big for my mouth. Maybe we were storing them for a friend.

If we were then they had obviously forgotten about them. The sticker on the lower plate had October 92 stamped on it, so they were well past by their wear by date.

As I uncovered more unrecognisable items I began to wonder if we had been hoarding other people's junk. Most of our furniture is antique so there was always the possibility that I was digging down through at least a century of communal clutter.

This made binning the stuff even easier.

At first my plan was to fill bags with stuff until they threatened to explode and then lug them warily out to the end of the pend and dump then in the bin. Twice the bags burst before I got there and I had to chase frantic scraps of junk around the courtyard trying to catch them before they escaped into the neighbour's garden and claimed asylum.

Bringing the bin to the back door was my finest moment. Now I could empty entire drawers of uninspected rubbish without even leaving the house.

Anything that was obviously useful was added to the growing number of charity boxes and soon I began to feel lighter and revitalised. The therapeutic value of clearing out clutter should never be underestimated. It was like shedding an old skin.

The only problem was I couldn't move it. In my fevered state I'd also dragged the neighbour's bin round and filled that, but the weight was extraordinary.

With some difficulty I managed to cajole the bins back into the pend but decided I would have to tow them behind the car up to the end of the drive in the morning. Hopefully when the refuse men tried to pick them up I would be at work.

I was in the kitchen when I heard the rumble. It was Trevor our other neighbour dragging one of the wheelie bins slowly up the drive. He must have volunteered to put out the rubbish while the people next door were away. Although how they had filled a bin by proxy didn't seem to worry Trevor.

"Where's all the photographs of my thumb?" demanded my wife when she came back.

Needless to say when I told her Trevor threw them out to the bin men she didn't believe me.

The Pyjama Party

I can't remember falling asleep the first night in our cottage, but I do recall waking up and thinking I was on holiday, which I suppose I was.

I'd taken a week off to move house but that holiday feeling had more to do with the cottage itself, which reminds me of all the characterful little country houses we've rented in France and Italy.

So it seems to me a great thing if you can be at home and feel as if you're on holiday at the same time.

Anyone who visits you is treated accordingly, with a mixture of curiosity and amazement. The sort of welcome I normally reserve for tradesmen since in my experience most of them seem to forget about me the moment I hang up the phone.

The fact that the first visitors to our cottage were all tradesmen was doubly astonishing. I hadn't forgotten they were coming, but I must have forgotten where we were. In the country tradesmen seem to be like buses, they all come at once and of course they all know one another.

They even knew our postie who was deputising for another pal who was off with a bad back. Being half awake and still exhausted from the rigours of the move I could barely follow this three-way doorstep conversation but I was struck by the sudden realisation that everyone concerned, including myself had time for a 'newsy'.

It was refreshing if a little disarming. Standing outside in the boxer shorts and T-shirt that pass for pyjamas I did my best to blend in. Even when someone mentioned that it was a bit on the nippy side that morning I blithely stood my ground and sympathised knowingly with the trials and tribulations of the busy postie.

I recommended an acupuncturist and this led us even further away from the jobs in hand we were meant to be discussing. But I was as much to blame as my guests. The cottage and its idyllic setting had me under that holiday spell and I had moved into the crawler lane.

Chilled out is not an expression you would normally use to describe someone who had just moved house and who had woken up adrift in a sea of chaos but at that moment it fitted the bill.

So much so in fact that I had forgotten my wife was in the bathroom running herself a bath while all this was going on. Although it was probably just as well.

My wife isn't the sort of gal you can buy expensive nightwear for. I only once bought her silk pyjamas for Christmas and they were quickly transformed into cushion covers, so I took the hint.

The timber treatment bloke was next on the scene, although he seemed to be in too much of a hurry to stop. We watched him drive passed craning his neck at us and then he vanished up the road to the village.

Another van stopped and asked me for directions to a place that sounded as if it might be in deepest Devon. I explained to the driver that I had no idea where we were and he lifted an eyebrow at my boxers as he drove off down the road in time to pass the timber treatment bloke who sped passed us yet again.

By the time he made it back I was in detailed discussions with Andy the electrician and George the central heating engineer was doing mysterious things to the boiler.

I thought it was probably time for me to get organised in the trouser department, but first I had to find a pair. I had five apparently identical sealed wardrobe boxes to choose from. It was like a game show.

As I pointed out the positions of the sockets I wanted to Andy, I deftly worked my way through the boxes. After five minutes Andy was happy with the socket situation and I had a choice of a dark pinstripe suit, an overcoat I thought I had thrown out in 1985 and one of my wife's long striped cardigans.

It was a close thing but in the end I stuck with my makeshift pyjamas. At least George had the heating going.
Unfortunately he wanted to check something in the bathroom at the exact moment the timber treatment bloke wanted to fill his big container with water from the bath.

George said he could amuse himself elsewhere in the heating system and I promptly showed the timber treatment bloke into the bathroom.

"Oh good," he said, "the bath's running already."

I don't know what was more surprising, finding my wife standing in the bathroom or seeing her in a pair of large strange pyjamas, which despite the size she rather suited.

As I had hoped she was more interested in what the timber treatment bloke was about to do in the loft than the fact that she had been caught about to disrobe and enter her bath. She stepped forward boldly and introduced herself as if we were in a boardroom meeting.

The timber treatment bloke explained how he couldn't find our cottage and my wife sympathised telling him that it was a good job he didn't ask us for directions since we had no idea where we were.

"I have no idea where my clothes are either." she added laughing.

Andy poked his head in and started asking probing questions about the lights we wanted in the kitchen so the three of us trooped through and met George as he appeared as if by magic apparently from inside the boiler.

"That was a neat trick," announced my wife and then said hello to George.

Then it was all lights and circuits and more sockets while George tried to show us how to programme the boiler and the timber treatment bloke asked us how to get into the loft above the back room.

"Have we got a back room?" asked my wife thoughtfully.

"We must have." I answered beginning to wonder how many conversations I could handle before I started talking to myself. Hopefully someone was taking notes.

It was only a matter of time I thought before my wife started making tea for everyone, if she could find the tea.

Instead she decided she would get on with her bath so George followed her into the bathroom to check the cistern and Andy joined them with some more probing questions about the funky wall heater we had inherited.

It was quite a party. When they left we had about an hour before the next round with the decorator and the builder. Just enough time for my wife to have her bath and slip on that long cardigan I had found earlier.

"So where did you find the pyjamas?" I asked, thinking they had come with the cottage.

"Oh they're my brother's pyjamas," answered my wife laughing.

"So they've got a fly?" I asked.

That wiped the smile from her face.

Obviously it was more of a pyjama party than either of us had first thought.

Unsurprisingly the decorator and builder were early.

Lock Out

I had a powerful premonition of disaster the moment I unscrewed the handles from our porch door. Either that or it was just common sense, which makes a pleasant change.

So when I took the bolt out I laid it carefully on the inside window ledge and made a vivid mental note. It would be just typical of us to get ourselves locked inside the house I thought and told my wife as much.

She laughed and agreed that would be terrible. But since I was painting the door there was little chance of it being closed, particularly with us on the outside. Which would have been just as bad.

For a moment I tussled with that scenario, pictured myself struggling to climb in through a window or trying to open the door with a makeshift handle and decided to just leave the bolt where it was.

It was still a mini-crisis waiting to happen. But the main thing was; it wasn't going to happen to me. The day after I painted the door, I went off to buy new handles, so even if the door did shut I would be able to get back in.

"Remember not to close the porch door," I shouted on my way out.

"As if!" called back my wife, meaning of course, as if she would remember not to close the porch door, because that's exactly what she did.

About ten minutes after I left my wife suddenly remembered she had to go out and since it had started chucking it down she was concerned the porch was going to get soaked. So she closed the door.

I winced at this point when she later recounted her horrible adventure.

"Now hold a minute," she said her eyes widening, "I'm not as daft as you think you know. I didn't just close the door and hope for the best!"

I waited to be convinced and was duly impressed.

Apparently she had made sure she could open the porch door again by sticking her car key into the bolthole and successfully manoeuvring the snib.

Not when the door was closed of course that wouldn't have made sense and not with the bolt which was still lying on the window ledge, but had somehow managed to make itself invisible.

"And do you know what?" she asked hands now firmly on her hips.

"Your car key wouldn't open the door when it was shut," I said.

"How did you know that?" she demanded, but instead of waiting to find out how I knew the car key wasn't going to work she took me deeper into her nightmare of lock-out hell.

It was a weird and sometimes strangely wonderful story and if nothing else confirmed my belief that my wife is one of the most ingenious and determined people I know.

The reason she found out her car key wouldn't open the porch door so quickly was because the moment she closed it she realised she hadn't actually locked the main front door.

So there was nothing else for it, she just had to open the porch door otherwise she would have left our cottage wide open for any passing burglar to stroll in and help himself.

The chances of this happening were as remote as our cottage, but as my wife said, as long as there's a chance.

This burglar was obviously going to be able to open the porch door a lot easier than my wife. In fact if he had turned up about half an hour into her reverse escape she probably would have been absolutely delighted to see him.

Thinking about burglars her first move was to attempt to climb in through the top of the back room window which was open a tantalising few inches.

There was a report a few weeks ago about a monkey that was burgling houses and pinching mobile phones. I doubt if even that petite felon would have been capable of such a tight squeeze.

Although if he'd been around my wife would have probably dropped him down the chimney she was so desperate. Particularly when she discovered her head and shoulders were stuck though the window and she remembered we had painted the window frame that very morning. It wasn't wet, just tacky enough to give my wife a faint white chinstrap.

At this point I would have driven to the nearest DIY shop and bought a pair of handles, instead my wife decided she could make her own. She said it came to her as she was trying to pull herself free of the sticky window. Actually she landed on a clothes peg which she feverishly pulled apart.

She was smirking all the way to the porch door until she discovered the broken clothes peg still wouldn't fit. Undeterred she marched down to our summer house and after failing to find a knife started whittling away at the clothes peg with a pair of garden shears.

I had almost glazed over at this point, but her next brainwave pulled me back into the story with a look of stunned amazement.

Realising that there was little chance of her trimming the clothes peg with any accuracy she began hunting around the summer house for anything that resembled a door handle bolt.

She must have found something because she paused for dramatic effect and that smirk was back on. Obviously I was meant to guess what she had found but I was hungry and this was turning into an epic so I gave up.

She disappeared for a moment and returned proudly holding up a table lamp.

Even with a wild and painful stretch of my imagination I couldn't see how a table lamp could be deemed useful to your average burglar, not unless he needed to shed some light on the subject.

"The plug," said my wife, "Look at the plug!"

"Ah, right, the plug." I said, after a moment. Potentially the plug's biggest pin could have passed for a door bolt. The problem was how to get the plug unscrewed without a screwdriver.

This is where our secateurs came in. Briefly admittedly. Apparently you can unscrew a plug with the point of our secateurs, handy to know if I ever get stuck for a screwdriver.

Unfortunately the small screws inside proved more of a problem. So my wife marched back up to the porch with the plug still attached to the table lamp and shoved the big pin into the bolthole in the door.

When it didn't work she whipped out her car key and slipped it in beside the plug pin. At which magical point a country bus trundled passed and slowed down just long enough to allow its passengers an uninterrupted view of a crazed half-painted woman breaking into a house with a rather chic table lamp.

The moment she was inside the porch the bolt made itself visible again and it was all my wife could do not to throw it out across the garden after the bus.

The main front door of course was locked all along. That goes without saying because my wife is very security conscious.

The Joyrider

Rather than think the worst when she discovered her car had vanished my wife concocted a lovely little fantasy involving her father going for a spontaneous joyride.

Even though he has no history of joyriding or car jacking – that we know of, and is comfortably in his mid-seventies my father-in-law came up as the number one suspect.

Ripping through the countryside at a bunnet rattling 10 mph he had probably burned an iridescent trail across the parish that would be the talk of the post office queue for months.

It was an open and shut case. Even when my wife spotted her little blue car parked rather nervously at the bottom of the road fifty yards from her parents' house she decided it was probably still the work of her father.

Perhaps he had borrowed it she reasoned, to visit a neighbour down the road and she hurried into the house to confirm her suspicions.

"Joyriding!" shouted her father, blasting his pipe across the living room.

Apparently he was not amused by the accusation, in fact he was visibly bemused and decidedly disturbed by the fact that my wife's innocent looking car had been the source of so much local drama and near disaster.

The dust had now settled but there was still time for a reporter to turn up and transform the incident into a front-page headline like; 'Nobody Hurt in Driverless Car Incident".

My wife had to sit down to hear this one, particularly since it was obviously all her fault, even though she was somewhere else at the time.

Because it was such a nice afternoon she had left her car parked outside her parents' house and walked the mile or so into the village centre to do some errands.

It was a very pleasant walk, my wife had a spring in her step because the sun was shining, flowers were in bloom and the birds were in full song. She laughed at other people in their cars as she revelled in the tranquil fresh air.

By the time she reached the shops she felt thoroughly uplifted and at one with the world but while she was browsing blithely round the charity shops her car was stealthily lurching into life and was about to make a clean brake of it.

If my father-in-law had passed his front room window at that very moment he would have been surprised to see the tiny car sliding silently backwards down the hill towards the newly built wall of an elderly couple who had recently moved in.

Since the old gentleman in question was pottering happily around in his front garden just behind that wall, he was about to get a bulls-eye view.

Fortunately as the car trundled towards the wall it had a last minute change of heart.

All the same it must have been a trouser changing moment for the elderly gentleman as he glanced up from his gardening to see an unmanned vehicle reversing steadily into his property and then at the very moment of impending impact turning sharply away.

He was rendered speechless at the time but had a few words to say on the subject when my wife turned up to apologise.

As you can imagine she was absolutely shocked and horrified at the idea of almost having a car accident while she was buying someone's unwanted 1970's wedding presents.

In her defence she insisted that she had fully engaged the handbrake when she parked the car and never for one moment imagined that it might turn into such a dangerous missile.

She went on to explain how it had been in the garage the day before and although it was booked in for some work they assured her it was safe to drive. Obviously as the old chap pointed out, it wasn't safe to park.

Although it was now sitting on a perfectly flat road he wasn't taking any chances and had wedged a brick firmly behind one of the back wheels.

My wife apologised again and congratulated him on his ingenuity, then asked if she could keep the brick – in case she needed to park later, she was planning on going to the bank and it was on quite a steep hill.

"I think he thought I was a bit of a loony." She reflected later as she recounted the horror story. "He gave me a such funny look."

"Really," I sympathised, "there's just no pleasing some people."

I was just happy I wasn't there when her father's pipe blew across the room, even metaphorically.

I was even happier I wasn't around a few weeks later when my wife tried to put things right with the brick man.

Probably because she spent so many years as a pedestrian my wife fully appreciates the value of a friendly lift in the rain. She'll often eye up complete strangers caught in a downpour and suggest we stop and give them a lift. Unfortunately at this point I'm always overcome by temporary deafness.

However, since she was on her own when she spotted the brick man and his wife struggling home through a gale force rainstorm with only a shredded brolly between them she felt it was the ideal opportunity to make amends.

Unfortunately the soaked couple were on the other side of the road so my wife sounded her horn as she passed them. They stopped and looked back as she drove on and my wife was happy she had got their attention.

But by the time she had turned the brick man's wife had already crossed the road with her brolly leaving her husband to the mercy of the elements and more importantly my wife.

When she stopped and asked if he lived in such and such an avenue he motioned ahead through the driving rain thinking my wife was lost and asking for directions. He was obviously getting wetter by the second so my wife decided there was no time to waste.

She threw open the passenger door and told him to jump in but he just stepped back and shouted something to his wife, it may have been "help!"

Undeterred my wife persisted saying that she knew where he lived and told him again to hop in without delay because she was going the same way, even although she was now pointing in the opposite direction.

He looked at her wide-eyed with disbelief, and peered into the car. For a moment my wife thought she had him, but convinced he was either being picked up by a desperate woman half his age or kidnapped he legged it across the road throwing worried glances over his shoulder.

When my wife passed the couple again she slowed down and saw brick man pointing her out to his bedraggled wife, so she thought she'd better leave them to it and drove on.

"It was such a shame," said my wife later, "They looked so wet and miserable, but the poor chap obviously didn't recognise me."

But I reckon he did recognise her and the car. The brick on the backseat was probably a give-away.

Flies Are Us

My wife reckoned it wasn't a good idea keeping a pet that threw up on our breakfast.

She can be very practical when she likes.

But Boris the fly had been around for so long I felt he was almost part of the family. He certainly showed no sign of spreading his wings and heading for the great fly infested outdoors, in fact he was remarkably loyal.

He was there when I left in the morning, grooming himself in front of the bathroom mirror and he was buzzing around the hallway when I returned in the evening waiting to pounce the moment I came through the door.

He was even there when we came back from our trip to Amsterdam, hovering in patient expectation of his present – a clog over the head.

Unfortunately apart from our never ending games of hi-speed hide and seek, which admittedly were immense fun and an excellent way for both of us to keep fit, we never seemed to spend any real quality time together.

Except of course when we sat and watched Jeff Goldblum in the remake of The Fly, which was a thoroughly bonding experience.

"I think Boris and I should get a lot closer." I announced to my wife as she waved her arms around the kitchen in a vain attempt to convince Boris she was a martial arts expert.

"Good, idea," she declared, "then you can kick his bacteria laden ass!"

She was right of course; each house fly can easily carry over one million bacteria on its body and a quick calculation proved it was more than likely that Boris' ass was indeed bacteria laden.

And anyway while he was throwing up on our breakfast, he was probably taking a dump on it at the same time. He was bad company, and he had to go.

But that was easier said that done. Apparently when flies enter a house they automatically make a mental note of how they got in – which makes sense when you think about it because if they didn't there would be no flies outside.

But either Boris wasn't as bright as his mates or he just got too cosy. Either way he had to be shown the door, preferably head on like a speeding bullet.

As our games of chase and hide and seek intensified Boris seemed to grow smarter, leaner and faster. His fly swat radar became so acutely honed that I just had to think about pouncing and he was off like a tiny fighter jet ready to open fire on my lunch.

If nothing else living with Boris must have done wonders for our immune system.

About a fortnight after he arrived Boris decided to test that notion by moving in his entire family, in fact he moved every fly in the neighbourhood into our little cottage and that's when we began to wonder if we were living in Flies Are Us.

When we bought the cottage we couldn't help noticing the delicate transparent sunflowers stuck to the windows. For weeks I thought they were a quaint colourful decoration, like the hanging stained glass designs you see in some houses.

The sunflower stickers were rather faded and it wasn't until we looked really close at one of them that we read the words, 'Fly Killer'.

Then we noticed some of our neighbours also had them. "Oh," said my wife nervously, "There must be flies here."

There certainly were, and most of them were in our house. Our white walls didn't help, but since a redecoration in fly black was out of the question it was time to find out who was the real Lord of the Flies.

For at least another week it was Boris. He reigned supreme over his hordes as I threw my right shoulder out of joint trying to wipe the smirk off their collective faces with my specially selected rag.

It had a particularly satisfying whiplash factor, but it was still very much a hit or a miss, mostly a miss.

Then my wife hid the vacuum cleaner. Obviously she must have spotted some familiar tell-tale sign.

Years ago when we were not long married and my wife still trusted my judgement I had a brainwave that involved hoovering up all the flies that were annoying us. I actually sat in the middle of the room and pointed the vacuum nozzle at any fly that crossed my path and sucked them up. It was wonderfully successful.

I was quite proud of my ingenuity until I got a panic phone call at the office from my wife screaming something about the cupboard we kept the vacuum in being infested with maggots. Now of course I appreciate the simple biology involved, but as my wife knows, it's difficult to teach an old dog new tricks as far as flies are concerned.

Which is why she turned up with a scaled down modern version of my original concept. When I reminded her that I had come up with the idea in the first place more than twenty years ago she just said that at least I would know how to use it. So I didn't ask.

It looked to me like a miniature Star Wars light sabre so off I went with gritted teeth to do battle with the dark forces of the menacing Boris and his cohorts.

It wasn't much of a success. In fact I would have been better trying to suck the flies up through a straw. The aperture was so small you had to be deadly accurate and if you didn't keep the suction on your captive literally walked free.

"I think you have to kill the flies first." Remarked my wife as I swivelled around on top of the coffee table sucking up nothing but air.

So we bought some more sunflower window stickers and Boris and his pals finally moved out of the house and found a new residence.

"Oh look," chorused a group of passengers in my car one day, "You've got loads of flies."

I had to let them out in the end so they could walk the rest of the way home. The flies stayed on for the ride.

By this time I was demented so when I arrived at the cottage and found the living room walls plastered with miniature replicas of Boris I went a bit Jeff Goldblum.

"They won't live long," said my wife calmly as I thrashed around filling up my light sabre with hundreds of fluttering flylets.

"Don't worry," I shouted back, "I'm working as fast as I can!"

It was dark outside but against the living room window I could clearly see a smoke screen of little flies thrashing at the glass to get in, so I rapidly emptied the fly sucker and jumped back into the house.

Two minutes later my wife was applying the sucker to what can only be described as my beastie heid.

From now on we're going to walk around in muslin tents. My wife's already done a few preliminary designs. If nothing else we might frighten the flies to death.

Stinky

As chief windbreaker in our house I seldom get the chance to point the accusing finger. So when I arrived home and bumped into a wall of silent but deadlies, I thought, aha, at last a serious bid for my title.

In fact it was so serious I was rendered speechless, although to be honest I think I was just too scared to open my mouth.

Eventually I managed to squeeze out my hellos and then ask my wife if there was something she wanted to tell me.

And of course there was, all very interesting and entertaining stuff, but none of it even remotely connected with the world of stink we were now inhabiting. Our cottage is very small so it only took a few seconds to check every room.

"I bet it's even in the loft," I said too loudly, fanning my way across our bedroom.

My wife stopped punishing some vegetables and popped her head out of the kitchen door.

"Terrible isn't it," she shouted, "It's putting me off my tea, and I'm starving."

"It's certainly thorough." I shouted back as I was quickly repelled from the linen cupboard.

"What do you think it is?" asked my wife chopping away. "It must be coming in from the fields." She added, but I just laughed quietly to myself and said nothing. I had just opened the wardrobe and face was now too screwed up for speaking.

After a moment or two when the penny finally dropped my wife was out in the hallway with that big vegetable knife in her hand.

"You don't think it was me?" she asked looking suitably shocked.

I just stared at her and smiled feebly. "Did you have stinky visitors?" I asked.

"The smell's obviously coming from outside," she insisted aloofly and went back to her vegetable slicing. "Honestly, when have I ever done anything like that?" she tutted.

"You could have been saving it up." I shouted then held my breath as I closed the wardrobe. "Actually I'm quite proud of you, it's a worthy effort." I continued reeling back from the aftershock.

The next thing I knew we were standing outside, me half-dressed, and my wife holding me by the scruff with that big knife still in her hand.

They must time the country bus round our area to drive very slowly past just when the action's hotting up at our cottage.

It's probably printed in the bus timetable: 10.30am Mrs Phillips attempts to open her porch door using a three pin plug which is still attached to a table lamp, 1.00pm Mr Phillips stands unsteadily on top of the roof wearing a suit and helps the aerial fitter by pointing at distant landmarks, 6.30pm the couple unite in their garden for a self-defence demonstration.

The bus caught us frozen at the top of a deep intake of fresh air. Just as well because I was beginning to feel sick.

My wife now looked suitably baffled, I thought she had rescued me from the world of stink but she had actually been trying to prove her innocence. All her evidence however, had been blown away into someone else's house.

"The wind must have changed," she said frowning and sniffing the air suspiciously.

It sure had, I thought to myself and went inside and threw open all the windows so hundreds of flies could fill the house.

Still, I like a challenge and just after five in the morning I thought I had risen to it. You wouldn't think a smell could wake you from a deep sleep but this one did. I can't remember what I was dreaming about, but the otherwise completely benign dream was slowly invaded by a horrible stink. Someone, probably me, asked if there was a doctor in the house and then I dragged myself awake convinced I was the guilty party.

I remember thinking I had gone a bit too far this time as I opened another window, only to discover that my wife had been right, the stink was coming from outside.

Once I had hermetically sealed the house I went back to bed and drifted off to sleep nursing images of sulphur mines. In the morning my wife had decided I was the owner of the mines.

"What happened to, 'oh it's coming from outside?" I asked. But apparently that was a different, much healthier farmyard pong, although how a smell can be particularly healthy I have no idea.

The rather large matter of my previous record was held up in evidence against me and I had to agree there was a chance I could be the guilty party. Although if I was then I had surpassed myself and medical advice should be sought.

However, the stink debate was quickly settled that same evening. A quarter of a mile from our cottage I drove into it in its full glory and nearly went off the road. I was convinced however that I would drive through it, but it was waiting for me in the garden when I got out of the car.

In the house, my wife's face was permanently asked from taking short little breaths out of the side of her mouth. But I must have grown used to it because out I marched out after tea to sand down some old furniture at the bottom of the garden.

After an hour or so I had convinced myself it smelled like plasticene and a raft of primary school memories, some more pleasant than others buoyed me along. Although it could have just been the fact that I was wearing a mask while sanding.

My wife appeared and decided to start priming the sanded furniture with the stinkiest paint she could stick a brush in. And so began the short lived war of the pongs.

Wiping down the table top and chairs with turps was a valiant assault, which we spun out as long as we could. Once the allure of plasticene memory lane had worn off I resorted sniffing the paintbrush I was using but even that quickly wore off.

In the end my wife found some bright green foam earplugs and we stuck them up our noses. Bliss, if a little on the waxy side. After about ten minutes my wife decided we should swap earplugs. "I think I've got yours." She said.

It's always just a matter of time before a car being driven by someone with a scrunched up map stops at Lost Corner. This time it was a couple looking for a cottage that was for sale a few of miles up the road.

"It's a lovely area." Said the bloke.

I nodded in agreement, then assured him it didn't always smell as bad and that the culprit was probably a field that had been spread with muck. He looked relieved, then turned to his female passenger saying, "Told you it wasn't me."

She didn't seem convinced, obviously he had something of a reputation. I knew the feeling.

"Come on stinky, back to work." Shouted my wife. When the couple drove off they looked genuinely scared.

Pump Up The Volume

If you want a bath round our house you have to start running it the night before. Running being a gross exaggeration. The hot water limps reluctantly from the tap as if it's got a better offer.

"Honestly," said my wife one evening as she sat on the edge of the bath utterly transfixed by the thread-like trickle, "you'd think it was doing us a favour. If it wasn't for us it would be just plain old cold water."

She was raving but she had a point. After going to all the trouble and expense of heating the water you would have thought it would have had the decency to turn up.

The casual couldn't care less hot water supply has come at a bad time for me. I gave up wallowing in my own diluted dirt a few years ago, basically because I used to bob off in the bath and I wasn't convinced it was the sort of thing that had long term prospects. So I decamped to the shower and became a slave to its instant gratification.

When we moved to our cottage my wife persuaded me back into my old bathing habits because the shower wouldn't go off after you had used it. Turning the water off at the mains seemed a touch extreme so we put the shower on our 'Someone'll Fix It' list and I went for a soak in the bath.

It wasn't long before I realised what I had been missing, mainly damp books and skin shrivelled and puckered like a prune. But this I reckoned was a small price to pay for an hour of scented candle bliss.

The only drawback about the bath was the noise. Baths are meant to be peaceful relaxing affairs designed to help you wind down from the turmoil of the day. In our house the word bath was a euphemism for 'run for cover!'

"I'm just going to have a bath!" my wife would shout and then give me five minutes to get clear. Otherwise I would get hit by the phantom express train that thundered through the cottage for about five minutes, rattling the windows and floorboards and generally jangling our nerves to screaming point.

The same thing happened when we flushed the toilet. If we did it in the dead of night the entire village down the road must have leapt from their beds in alarmed unison.

This racket was so all encompassing it took us two weeks to pin it down to somewhere vaguely in the loft and even then we weren't convinced. When we opened the little cupboard in the front room the noise was so scary it made us duck, even though the cupboard was empty.

"Maybe it's a ghost train!" declared my wife over the din.

Personally I came to the conclusion that even if it was a ghost train I was going to jump on it and get as far away as possible. It was the one blot on our otherwise idyllic rural life and for some reason we thought we could live with it, or rather my wife did.

"Just ignore it!" she would shout, "after a few months you won't even notice it. It'll just become part of your environment, part of your comfort zone. In fact when you're at work you'll probably miss it."

My wife is good at wishful thinking and sometimes it can be highly infectious. But in this instance I was willing to resist it.

The steaming hot water roared out though in a furious torrent and filled the bath in about two minutes.

"It must be the pressure, it's obviously far too high," I declared managing to sound so knowledgeable I almost convinced myself.

There was certainly pressure, particularly if you were running a bath and happened to flush the toilet at the same time. The overhead train took off like a bullet and ran from room to room then crashed somewhere above the kitchen. Fortunately there were no reported injuries, but it must have given the mice a run for their money.

Just when you thought the dust had settled the engine began hissing and started up again, and chugged slowly all the way back.

The first visitors to our cottage sat mesmerised over their cups of coffee, gazing anxiously at the ceiling while we chatted away pretending nothing was happening. They never mentioned it and have never been back.

Eventually I have to say the novelty wore off and we called in George our favourite central heating engineer.

True to his trade George loves a mystery. When I gave him a demo by flushing the loo he stood there with his fists on his hips glowering darkly up at the ceiling.

"What do you think George?" I asked hopefully once the racket had subsided.

"Well," he began scratching his chin, "I would say there's a loud noise coming from your loft."

At least we hadn't imagined it, I thought. Far from it, after a brief foray in the loft George returned with a strange tale about a big shower pump bouncing around on the joists. He also confirmed my own earlier diagnosis.

"It's your water pressure," he said, wiping his hands, "it must be really low."

But why a shower pump? George just gave an enigmatic smile and gazed back up at the ceiling. That was the bit he liked, that was the mystery.

Until such time as the mystery was solved I went up into the loft and cushioned the shower pump so that it now sounded like a cement mixer wearing a big coat.

Or at least that's how the bloke from Scottish Water described it.

"It was more a big train thing we had going before," I said helpfully.

Just to add to the mystery he checked the water pressure at the front of the cottage and told me we really had nothing to worry about because it was actually high enough to blow the roof off the house. Fortunately it was held firmly in check. He only added this after seeing the stark look of horror on my face.

"And the pump will have to go I'm afraid," he continued, "it's supplementary to requirements."

"Oh that's a shame," I lied and ran back into the house rubbing my hands with glee.

Apparently the pump had been installed when the cottage's water came from a nearby well, but that had all changed now with the arrival of the roof erupting mains supply.

So George came back and removed the shower pump and peace reigned in the little cottage. Until my wife ran a bath and became mesmerised by the stubborn trickle from the hot tap.

The patient bloke from Scottish Water returned and said it was something to do with the Combi boiler and the size of the pipes.

"I'm afraid you can't have one without the other," he mused, "but look on the bright side you've got enough potential water pressure coming in to drive the house all the way to John o' Groats."

Which gives us something to think about while we're waiting for the bath to fill I suppose.

The Post

Once you've had your garden re-designed by livestock you would think there would be very little left that could surprise you.

The six dairy cows in question were big on earth churning and weed clearing but lacked a little flair in the landscaping department.

Still it was a worthy if impromptu effort and the farmer was full of apologies. It didn't bother us; it was just a fact of country life. You can't gaze longingly out onto a field of central casting dairy cows for nothing.

So we were 'cool'. In fact everyone was 'cool' apart from the cows that had, I imagine been very much on the anxious side at finding themselves surprise guests on The Great Escape.

Unfortunately my cool lasted about a week after which I promptly lost it in a flash when I turned into our drive and happened to notice the three foot high wooden post that had miraculously appeared from nowhere and stuck itself into our mossy bank.

I couldn't remember seeing it before and I certainly didn't grow it but there was no denying it was there.

I then did exactly the same thing I did when I discovered our garden had been used as the set for Bonanza; I stood with my hips on my hands and glanced around frowning. Nobody ever appears from behind a bush shouts 'ha ha I did that' and then runs off, but it's always worth a try.

Even when I shouted 'what flipping next?' there were no takers, only birdsong and the rumble of a distant tractor.

For a moment I actually began to wonder if the bank and the drive belonged to someone else, and the wooden post was the beginning of a fence that would eventually keep us in, or out, depending on when it was finished.

The post had definitely come to stay; in fact it was rock solid so it was unlikely it had just blown in accidentally, but you never know.

My father used to say that stranger things happened at sea, but that was just because he never lived in the country.

I gave the rest of the garden a quick scout but as far as I could see the post was on its own. Simmering nicely I marched up to the house and remembered Andy the electrician was re-wiring the kitchen so I was hoping he could shed some light on the matter, he usually does, quite literally.

But he was nowhere to be seen, which meant he was in the loft.

I needed someone to sound off about the post so I phoned my wife who was equally baffled.

"Why didn't he just put it through the letterbox?" she said making me frown even harder.

"Who?" I asked trying to unknot my brain.

"The postman," she replied as if I didn't have a brain to unknot.

We still get letters for everyone who ever lived in our cottage from before the Great War and recently its turned into the mail sorting office for the village, but delivering all those bills is actually quite therapeutic.

My wife had obviously got hold of the wrong end of the post so when I told her it was a wooden one she asked what it was for, and when I said I had no idea she assured me that I would think of something.

We left it that.

By the time Andy appeared from the loft he could see I was rather unhappy at the idea of someone staking a claim on my garden because he backed away from me, even though he was holding something very sharp and horrible.

"Nothing to do with me!" he said, "it was the farmer, something to do with keeping the cows out of your garden."

Eventually when I had stopped ranting about how I might have wanted to put up a pair of big flashy Dynasty style gates and I ran out of ways to complain about having a big wooden post appear suddenly at the bottom of my drive, Andy broke the news about the other one.

"Well of course there's two," he laughed, "where else would you put the other end of the big blue nylon rope?"

"Oh that sounds nice," I said, but I think Andy could sense my insincerity.

Apparently the farmer said he would leave me a note, but I never had a chance to look for it because Andy decided it was time for me to become his apprentice again so up we went into the loft.

Even though I partially floored the loft I can't get excited about a place that's hot, airless and stuffed with fibre glass wool. Andy on the other hand has spent a lot of time in our loft over the past three months and seems to have made himself quite at home.

He was darting back and forth like Spiderman while I mindlessly pulled a variety of wires. At one point I thought I was working him, but I think it was the other way round.

He had been patiently listening to me whining on and muttering darkly about the post when suddenly he picked up my old guitar, sat down with it on his knee and began to play it, strumming out some gentle harmonious chords.

"The fact is, " he began sagely, "You need something to block your drive when they're moving the cows back and forth and the farmer has very kindly done the job for you, and a good job he's done too by the sound of it."

I had to agree with that, but I was getting very hot sitting listening to Andy's calming words of wisdom and his soothing moves on the fretboard.

"Anyway," he continued, "if you paint then the same dark green as your fence you'll never see them."

He was right again and he still hadn't hit a bum note, but I was beginning to get restless.

Normally when someone picks up a guitar that's lying around they hit a few chords and put it down, but Andy just kept playing.

How surreal is this, I thought, I'm stuck in a hot loft with an electrician who I'm paying to serenade me on my own guitar. You just couldn't make up stuff like that.

For a minute or two I found myself nodding along to Andy's beguiling tune. It was a Sound of Music moment, but suddenly that wooden post flew back into my head

"Enough guitar!" I shouted and pulled the thing off him.

By the time my wife arrived I had remembered what a big fan I was of Bonanza. I had also decided I was rather pleased to be an important part of the farmer's world, I was in his gang and anyway, no one else seems to have their own private cow guard.

"Oh it's a lovely post and its even the same green as our fence," enthused my wife, "hh and there's two of them, is that a spare?"

I haven't told her about the blue nylon rope. As chief cow guard operator I think that will be my job.

Hair Raising

I woke up one morning last week with my ideal hairstyle. At first glance I just assumed I was seeing things. I usually am when I've just woken up, the world just floats in front of me like a collection of bleary half-baked shapes.

Which is just as well. I'm also one of those vague spectre-like forms so my temporary myopia must be nature's way of easing me into the day. Otherwise I would never get out of the house.

Normally I wake up with a different hairstyle, some more extraordinary than others but essentially none of them could be worn in public, not unless you were in the circus. I don't mind my hair going a bit haywire when I'm out, but I think it's good to start out with the best intentions.

This involves nothing more than persuading my hair into a sensible shape. It has a life of its own, in fact it has a whole career based around the concept of standing up on end. So it needs restrained, which I've become very good at.

It was so lively at one point that my wife recommended I wear a hairnet in bed, a passion killer if ever there was one. Some days I used to wish I had taken her advice.

At the slightest hint of dampness I turned into Coco the clown. I could go to work with a normal hairstyle, or at least normal by my standards and just a few hours later I would be walking around with an Afro. It was a source of constant amazement and amusement.

Then my hair went all manic-depressive. One day it would be high as a kite the next it could barely get itself out of bed. Its unpredictability was the only predictable thing about it.

For a time I used to wonder if it was a physical manifestation of my inner self, but my wife reckoned I just had barmy hair. Which is the same thing.

Recently it's given up the ghost and lost the will to live altogether and I yearn for it's for its hilarious brush impressions.

"My hair doesn't work anymore," I complained to my wife, "I think I've broken it."

"It's just part of the ageing process," she answered sagely, "you should be thankful you're not a woman."

How many times have I nodded along in agreement to that one?

The trouble is, my hair must be ageing at a different rate from the rest of me, because for the past few months I've had old mannie hair. Wispy fluff that can't be bothered making an effort anymore and wants to hide under a bunnet at green bowling matches.

"Look, here's your doppleganger," announced my wife one evening pointing at some geezer called David Dickinson who presents the TV programme Bargain Hunt. I think she was trying to cheer me up, but it didn't work.

"Flipping heck!" I shouted, "don't tell me I'm turning into him, he's a male impersonator."

Apparently I already had the suit and the hairstyle to match, a sort of latent mullet that's evolving into a giant conch shell of candyfloss. All I needed was some chunky gold jewellery from Argos anda burnt umber spray tan.

Obviously when this bloke looks in the mirror he sees a wicked coif on his napper. He bounces back convinced he is a cool lady magnet of immense pulling power. Apparently he's had the same hairstyle since 1969 and his mother was a hairdresser, but that's still no excuse.

I went immediately into the bathroom to check out the resemblance. My wife had a point about the hair, although I hadn't brushed it for a whole day, just sort of shoved it around and propped it back up again. And I do like a bargain.

So that was that. A new hairstyle beckoned, or even Beckhamed.

This was a big step for me because I've never been in a hairdresser and I didn't think I could handle being held hostage by a scissors wielding stranger and being forced to discuss my holidays.

So my wife recommended trying her new hair straightening tongs, to remove what she called the natural kink in my troubled locks. So I plugged them in and after a quick demo it couldn't have looked easier. It certainly worked for my wife; her hair looks fit and glossy.

Once they got going the hair straighteners smelled suspiciously as if they were cooking my hair from the scalp out and I couldn't bear to watch so I didn't bother switching on the light.

There's a certain amount of peril involved using hair straightening tongs which my wife had of course warned me about, aside from being caught in the act by the postie. I had just burned my fingers for the third time when he came to the door with a parcel. I had only done one side of my head – I was trying to be methodical, so the postie eyed me up with a certain amount of interest.

"I'm between hairdos," I said, "haven't made up my mind which one to go for yet."

He nodded sympathetically and said I was lucky to have a choice in the first place.

When I went back to the mirror I thought I'd better switch the light on to see how my fashionable new hairdo was progressing. One half was still hanging about in a half-hearted wavy froth, but the other looked as if it belonged to David Carradine in Kung Fu, when he grows his hair of course, not when he's bald as a coot.

I had inadvertently realised a long cherished but forgotten dream. If it had been thirty years ago I would have been chuffed to bits. Instead I reckoned I looked like a reject muppet – too scary for the kids.

I gave my wife back her tongs and said I would be making my own arrangements. When she asked what they were exactly I told her I was going for the dishevelled bed head.

"Please yourself," she warned, "but it won't work with old mannie hair."

I got as far as the window of a trendy high street hairdresser with a mystical name where I stood and looked longingly at enlarged black and white photographs of male models with extra thick lovingly dishevelled hair.

There was just no way my hair would behave like that on a full time basis, so I went home to brush my Bargain Hunt barnet.

And then I woke up the next morning with that perfect hairstyle. My hair had obviously been listening.

"What do you think?" I said excitedly to my wife.

"Lost the hairbrush?" she asked briefly glancing up.

I stood there with the glummest face I could muster and caught myself in the mirror looking like a schoolboy up before the beak for not combing his hair for assembly.

"Look, just think of your hair as losing weight," she advised, "You've got lean hair and it's mean because it won't do what it's told."

Lean and mean I thought as I swaggered out into the merciless wind, now that's more like it.

The Workies

Darren said the digger was only a metre wide. So I immediately thought, how cute, a baby digger and then asked if I could get a 'shottie'. Perhaps not wanting to offend me I never really got a straight answer on that one.

No wonder. The digger Darren drove up our front steps and into the garden may have been just a meter wide but it was still a JCB and longer than my car. Surreal just wasn't the word for it, alarming would have done though.

I happened to be standing in the kitchen drinking a cup of coffee and staring mindlessly out of the window at the beguiling pastoral scene of fields and trees when the bucket with its huge metal teeth swung into view from round the corner.

It must have been the longest time I have ever stood with my mouth open. As luck would have it the sink caught most of my coffee as it trickled out of my cup.

Obviously the baby digger must have been sick I thought and sent his dad instead.

There had been some discussion about how exactly this baby digger was going to end up in our back garden to start work on the foundations for our conservatory. The fence I had just given three coats of paint might have to be temporarily dismantled but I didn't like the sound of that.

Even worse my favourite clematis which was entwined around the fence might also have to go, but I liked the sound of that even less.

"Not likely," I told Darren, "by all means come and build my conservatory for me but not over my dead clematis."

Darren was silent for a moment, obviously mulling over how much pain I was going to cause him, but he bounced back chirpy as anything and said he would give it some thought.

Knowing absolutely nothing about building work I immediately went into expert mode and recommended some kind of hoist assembly probably connected to a crane if a helicopter was going to prove too expensive. Or perhaps the digger could be dismantled and rebuilt in the garden. I even offered to lend a hand. After all how many parts could a baby digger have?

Darren decided he would just drive the digger up our steps, and that's what he was doing while I stood with my mouth open spilling my coffee into the sink.

The whole exercise only took five minutes but it seemed like an hour to me as Darren cajoled the snorting JCB through our gateway then round the impossibly tight corner onto the path. As the bucket swung closer to the kitchen window I swayed back and forth and actually ducked at one point.

When it finally ground to a halt I was so excited I was still alive and our cottage was intact I bolted outside to congratulate Darren on not killing me.

"No problem," he said, then glanced back over his shoulder at the steps, "tight fit though, should be fun getting it out."

I hadn't thought of that and suggested he just leave it in the garden when they were finished.

"I could make a feature out of it," I quipped, "grow an ivy up over it."

But Darren didn't think that was a good idea. The baby digger would probably get restless and start pining for all the holes it was meant to be digging in other people's gardens.

It certainly made a big enough one in ours.

"Maybe we should just tile it and turn it into a swimming pool." Reflected my wife as she stared into the abyss that now stretched before us to the back wall of our kitchen.

Quite what we expected to find when we arrived home at the end of the day I have no idea. Which was probably why we had spent the previous evening breaking sweat tidying and trimming the entire garden in preparation for our visitors. It looked an absolute treat when we had finished, so at least we had that memory to cling onto as we crept gingerly round the digger and the edge of the hole, then back across the great boards flattening our freshly cut grass.

"Oh well," I said, "You can't make an omelette..."

"Without breaking a garden." Butted in my wife.

"Don't worry," I said. "The worst bit is over."

The following afternoon my wife phoned to tell me the garden had been completely transformed. "Blimey, that was quick!" I shouted with delight.

"Transformed into a builder's yard." She added flatly.

Again, what did we expect? I think we had a vague notion that the conservatory fairy would come in the middle of the night and when we woke in the morning we would be able to have breakfast overlooking our pastoral idyll.

Instead it all seemed to be about the three M's, - murder, mystery and mayhem although not necessarily in that order. Not wanting to waste such an opportunity I took some photographs so I could frighten anyone who was considering having some building work done. After all, that's what friends are for.

The photographs would certainly have frightened me. The reality once we had surrendered to it was quite different, apart from being much bigger.

For a start I discovered how popular you become when your garden's a builder's yard. People in cars slowed down almost to a halt and suddenly our road was peppered with complete strangers out for a stroll.

The skip was probably the biggest crowd puller. When people see a skip they either want to know what they can get out of it, or what they can put in it, sometimes at the same time.

I even did it myself, pinching barrow loads of soil when Dougie the builder wasn't looking.

There was also something strangely exciting about having big strange stuff and chunks of serious machinery strewn about the garden. If I had been ten years old I would have been in my element. Although I didn't let that bother me.

After a few days I was out tidying up the garden in my overalls and playing at being workies. After a brief inspection of the work in progress I went out to the skip to steal some more of my own earth and a couple in a car slowed down as they passed.

I gave them a wave with my spade and I could see the woman nudging her husband as if to say 'why can't you be handy like him?'

When the foundations were laid I was almost sad to see the back of the big hole with its boulders the size of armchairs, some of which were so big they made even Dougie wipe his brow with amazement.

The baby digger cleared off without so much as a cheerio and now apart from the denouement of the doorway being knocked though the exterior wall into the kitchen all we've got to look forward to is the conservatory going up.

It's a sort of addictive rough magic having the builders in, only in the garden of course.

Gravel

I'm not a big fan of mud. My shoes on the other hand can't seem to get enough of it and mud having such a fondness for travel makes it the ideal companion for busy footwear.

Whenever anyone points at their floor and asks where all the mud came from I can tell them with complete confidence that it originated from the mudslide formerly known as our driveway.

Because it has a slight slope down to the road this driveway has been mulled over by a posse of chin scratching builders and landscape gardeners each of whom had a separate but similarly expensive method in mind for turning the drive into solid matter.

I heard the cases for Lock & Block, Tarmac and Cobbles but since none of the experts seemed particularly convincing we went for the easy option of mud. At least it was cheap.

When we moved into the cottage in April of course there was very little mud on the go, we had to wait patiently for it to churn up after the recent spates of continuous heavy rain.

At first it was just a tentative patch at the bottom of the garden steps, certainly not enough to make a song and dance over - you would have probably broken your neck, but more than enough to darken our doorway and our hallway.

A week of solid unrepentant rain that sounded on the conservatory roof like machine gunfire and the fields and roads were flooded and our drive looked like a Klondike mudslide.

The car wheels spun on it when I tried unsuccessfully to reverse up the drive and sprayed the apple trees with so much brown mud they looked as if they had been dipped in chocolate.

I cured it in an instant by throwing down some spare gravel, the very stuff everyone shook their head over because apparently it would run away.

Presumably when it was dark all the little granite chunks would pack their bags and make a dash for it. In the morning all that would be left would be a few straggling stick in the muds.

But even that was preferable to roping one another up just so we could get in and out of the car. My wife was going out to the local DIY store so after seven months of deliberation we made an executive decision in ten seconds and went for gravel. Five tons I reckoned after poking my head out of the door.

"But will that be enough?" asked my wife.

I shrugged and assured her it was impossible to measure mud, but it sounded a lot to me.

Unfortunately the sales assistant at the DIY store didn't agree.

"How Much?" she exclaimed in amazement.

Admittedly my wife had confused matters from the outset by asking the assistant how much gravel the small bags she had spotted in the yard contained.

When she was told they held 25kg she asked the woman how many bags she thought would fit in her car.

"Oh, nae very many dear," answered the assistant sucking air through the gap in her teeth.

For all the assistant knew my wife could have been driving a stretch limo. But that at least moved my wife onto the much bigger one ton bags.

"In that case I'll have five of those big bags of gravel please," announced my wife.

The assistant was visibly startled, frowned back at my wife then burst out laughing.
"Five o' yon big bags?" she exclaimed, "Oh no, ye dinna need five big bags, 'ats five tons, a dinna think so."

The assistant started sizing up my wife as if to work out her personal gravel capacity.

"No honestly," persisted my wife seeing miles and miles of mud stretching before her, "we definitely need five tons, maybe more."

The assistant took another deep breath and looked at her suspiciously, "fit's it for?" she asked, to which my wife gave her the life story of our mudslide and finished with a quick display of her muddied boots.

"Well, I've got a drive and I would only need half a ton," said the assistant matter of factly, "so ye dinna need five tons, nae unless ye live in Balmoral!"

"Maybe you're right," reflected my wife, "maybe I should just have four tons."

"Four tons!" laughed the assistant, "at's jist as bad, michty me four tons is a hale lorry load!"

It was only then it occurred to my wife that the assistant had no idea what size our drive was, the trouble was neither did my wife.

It was turning into a surreal sort of day. Earlier in a supermarket my wife had asked an assistant the time, she was worried that she might not get to the DIY store before it closed, and the assistant had replied, "what, like the time right now?"

"No the time in half an hour," replied my wife.

The woman in the DIY store decided it was time for reinforcements. Chuckling away to herself she put out a call for Dougie, the Gravel Master.

"Dougie'll sort ye oot," she said smugly as she put out another call.

My wife wasn't sure if she wanted sorted oot but when Dougie arrived sporting a friendly bunnet he seemed very avuncular and he looked sympathetic. He listened to both sides of the gravel story like Solomon and then scratching his chin at the assistant declared, "but hang on a minute, you dinna ken the size o' this lady's drive, it could be massive."

The assistant put her hands on her hips and narrowed her eyes at my wife.

"Is it massive?" she asked.

My wife thought for a moment, "not particularly," she replied hesitantly, shaking her head slowly.

"Telt ye," retorted the assistant back at Dougie, "it's nae massive and four tons is far too much."

But Dougie wasn't happy and wanted more information, "so fit size is yer drive dear?" he asked my wife, producing a pencil, obviously for a quick calculation.

My wife had now broken into a considerable sweat and was panicking at the mere thought of anything to do with real numbers so she explained that it was hard to tell the exact size of the drive because it was always covered in mud and both Dougie and the assistant stared at her in worried silence.

"So how much gravel can I have?" asked my wife eventually.

Dougie frowned again and thought deeply for a minute, glancing back and forth at the assistant who seemed to be prompting him with the right answer. My wife was about to ask if he would like to phone a friend when Dougie finally came up with the goods.

"Well, ye can hae four tons if ye like, but as lang as ye ken at's an affa lot o' gravel," he explained gravely.

"An affa lot o' gravel," chimed the assistant darkly, "a hale lorry load to be precise."

"Well that's what I would like," announced my wife confidently, "I'll have an affa lot of gravel please."

"Smashing!" declared the assistant and started ringing up the amount on the till.

"If it's too much can I take it back?" asked my wife nibbling at her nails.

Lost

I used to be a secret gardener, a closet potterer working undercover. Because we lived up a little country road and our huge garden was almost completely concealed by high thick trees no one saw me or my handiwork, except of course my family whose job it was to point out things I missed.

Sometimes, when the garden was looking particularly nice, when the wisteria and rhododendrons were in full bloom, I felt like opening it to the public, free of charge naturally. Our lawns were made for picnics. Basically our garden was a park with no visitors and I was the parkie with no pay.

So you can imagine my interest when a previous occupant of the little cottage we've just moved into told us how her husband had really enjoyed tending the garden because it was such a communal experience.

True, it took her several moments to find the word, 'communal' but it sounded like an attractive idea to me. Perhaps, I thought, coming over all misty-eyed, the whole village will turn out in Thomas Hardy smocks with scythes to help me tame the burgeoning bushes and briars.

Then we'll all sit under the Greenwood tree and quaff cider and cakes and one of the lads will start playing the accordion and there'll be dancing and merriment until dusk when a big cart will turn up and take everyone home still singing and laughing.

"Tell me when the squire turns up," interrupted my wife, "he's always devilishly handsome."

The first person who stopped while I was weeding the front garden was a grumpy bloke in an old white van. He had a squashed face, which may have explained why he was so grumpy; it certainly ruled him out as the squire.

"Hey pal!" he shouted, "where aboot's this?"

I looked around to check and told him with complete certainty that it was the place where my cottage was, which was obviously all he needed to know because he sped off.

It was the first time in years I had been interrupted from gardening by a passer by and I was probably a little under prepared. I made a mental note to do better next time. Which was just as well because less than five minutes later a people carrier packed with tiny old ladies stopped just inches from me.

A smiley old gent leaned out of the driver's window and pointed at the cottage.

"Wid 'at be the auld postie's hoose?" he asked.

He had me there. I told him it could have been but since I had not long moved in I couldn't verify it. I said he was welcome to have a look but as far as I knew there were no old posties in the house.

"Is at the postie's loon?" shouted one of the old ladies inside the people carrier.

"He's affa big!" shouted another.

"It's nae the postie's loon," shouted back the driver then turning again to me asked if I knew the auld postie, adding that he was really an auld 'postmaster'.

As fascinating as all this was I had to admit defeat. But not wanting to disappointment them I directed them to the post office.

"Nivir mind 'at," shouted one of the old ladies again, "how far's the nearest pub?"

I had no problem with that one.

Just as well I speak the language I thought, goodness knows what an inabootcomer would have made of that.

The following afternoon I got a chance to fully test my local knowledge when I set about the bank that spills out from the garden and down along the narrow country road. This is the stretch of garden our friend's husband found so communal. I could see what he meant. It wasn't long before my backside was communing with the country bus.

I was just regaining my senses when a bloke on a motorbike stopped beside me, lifted up his visor and asked me to point him in the direction of the remains of the meikle bogie.

Unfortunately I failed that one miserably. I burst out laughing and told him I was in no particularly hurry to become acquainted with the remains of any bogies, no matter how meikle.

I could have sworn he muttered 'toonser' as he pulled his visor back down, so I marched into the house and dug out a map of the area.

"He must have said the mains of Meikle something or other," assured my wife as we poured over the map.

"Look," I persisted, "if there's a big bogie nearby I think we should know about it, you don't want to drive into it one day by accident."

I never did find the meikle bogie but at least I now knew exactly where we were.

Lost Corner to be precise, because by that same evening that's where all roads seemed to lead.

I was strimming the verge back up at the front of the house when a young couple stopped and wearily asked if I could tell them where the 'toon' was. Obviously they were out of toonsers and just wanted any old toon.

They told me they had been driving around for hours and had forgotten what it was they were looking for.

"Everything looks the same," said the girl nursing a scrunched up map, which I assumed had been used to thump her partner who was now hugging the steering wheel.

"It's a' fields an bushes an trees..." she continued, glazing over.

I explained that was the general idea of the country and she just snarled to herself.

They were an easy case to solve. The next couple who roared up in an open top sports car looking for what sounded to me like Wester Cludgie weren't so lucky.

By this time I was growing weary of playing tour guide so I just pointed them in the first direction that came to mind and they sped off ripping a hole in the evening air.

I'm afraid the bloke in the Range Rover who addressed me as 'You there!' and asked for Achnapoodle got the same treatment.

You'd think that people on horses would know where they were going but maybe it's difficult to consult a map when you're trotting along on top of an animal. I took pity on horsie folk and went inside to get the map.

When I came back the horses were passing the time munching down the grass verge. But they were soon on their way and the dung came in handy for the flower beds.

To be fair there are no signs at our junction and it's nice to have company when you're gardening.

Most people stop outside the window of my wife's studio, or jail as we like to call it, so she plans to start selling ice-creams and soft drinks. I'm going to get some maps printed up and I've been working on a short but fascinating presentation on the history of Lost Corner. Our summerhouse would make a very nice tearoom and the garage an excellent gift shop.

At least everyone would be able to find us.

Until the next time...

Printed in Poland
by Amazon Fulfillment
Poland Sp. z o.o., Wrocław

51354122R00171